A Parents' ABC of the Autism Spectrum

of related interest

A Beginner's Guide to Autism Spectrum Disorders
Essential Information for Parents and Professionals
Paul G. Taylor
ISBN 978 1 84905 233 7
eISBN 978 0 85700 477 2

My Child Has Autism, Now What?
10 Steps to Get You Started
Susan Larson Kidd
ISBN 978 1 84905 841 4
eISBN 978 0 85700 349 2

Can I tell you about Autism?
A guide for friends, family and professionals
Jude Welton
Illustrated by Jane Telford
ISBN 978 1 84905 453 9
eISBN 978 0 85700 829 9
Part of the *Can I tell you about...?* Series

Can I tell you about Asperger Syndrome?
A guide for friends and family
Jude Welton
Illustrated by Jane Telford
ISBN 978 1 84310 206 9
eISBN 978 1 84642 422 9
Part of the *Can I tell you about...?* Series

A Parents'
ABC *of* the
Autism
Spectrum

Stephen Heydt

Jessica Kingsley *Publishers*
London and Philadelphia

First published in 2017
by Jessica Kingsley Publishers
73 Collier Street
London N1 9BE, UK
and
400 Market Street, Suite 400
Philadelphia, PA 19106, USA

www.jkp.com

Library of Congress Cataloging in Publication Data

Names: Heydt, Stephen, author.
Title: A Parents' ABC of the Autism Spectrum / Stephen Heydt.
Description: London ; Philadelphia : Jessica Kingsley Publishers, 2017. |
    Includes index.
Identifiers: LCCN 2016028295 | ISBN 9781785921643 (alk. paper)
Subjects: LCSH: Autism in children. | Autistic children--Care. | Parents of
    autistic children.
Classification: LCC RJ506.A9 H495 2017 | DDC 618.92/85882-
-dc23 LC record available at https://lccn.loc.gov/2016028295

British Library Cataloguing in Publication Data
A CIP catalogue record for this book is available from the British Library

ISBN 978 1 78592 164 3
eISBN 978 1 78450 435 9

Printed and bound in the United States

FOR PARENTS

There are no perfect parents.

For most children,
their parents are perfect.

Contents

For Parents

(Note: The terms autism, ASD and spectrum all have the same meaning in this book.)

This book contains wide-ranging information about children with Autism Spectrum Disorder. Every child with ASD is different, so while each subject will relate to some child, it may not be relevant to your child or any you may know or have met in the past. Throughout this book is information about children with ASD and the different ways in which they may think, feel and behave. The behaviour of different children and of any one child will vary, at times, from being unremarkable to being quite disruptive in any context, whether at home, school or in public. While a particular difficulty of the child may not be obvious and they may not have sufficient awareness of the difficulty or the communication skills for them to identify it to others, it does not mean that it is not present. For example, people with synaesthesia, an unusual and most interesting neurological condition with seldom any adverse consequences, do not realise until they talk about their own experiences that most people don't perceive a middle C in music as violet and B flat as smelling as roses or perhaps the letter H as pink and Q as tasting like nutmeg. This particular neurological difference is typically only diagnosed in adults, because children just don't realise that their sensations are any different from anyone else's. Similarly, when one person describes that they are anxious without clarifying they are scared of spiders, another person anxious at writing exams may make an incorrect assumption.

It is particularly important for children with ASD to have regular physical check-ups. Eyes, ears, sinuses, teeth, joints and stomachs should be examined at least every six months by an understanding and patient practitioner. Before any first visit by a child with ASD, parents should first have a discussion with the primary carer. For some reason, perhaps sensory insensitivity or high pain threshold, experience suggests that children with ASD do not seem to receive medical attention as quickly as their peers. Some individual examples: a child with chronic head-banging behaviour was found to have a badly rotten tooth, another with noise sensitivity had a middle ear infection, and a sweet ten-year-old had embarrassing public groin-grasping behaviour due, it was discovered, to a urinary tract infection.

This book is written from the perspective that any child, and all children with ASD, is as near perfect as humans can be. In much the same way as microscopic and sometimes significant differences add lustre or character, respectively, to the most beautiful diamonds, each child's different qualities enrich us all. In diamonds these differences are appropriately called 'inclusions'. Parents are little different from master diamond cutters; by working around the inclusions, with careful polishing and what in diamond cutting is marvellously called 'brillianteering', in their hands the most breath-taking jewels can emerge. Sadly, sometimes our inviolable systems of education shatter the jewel and leave it in a thousand pieces for someone else to attempt the repair. This book is written to assist you in forming those unique jewels.

This book gives some ideas that can be, and are recommended to you to be, implemented by you or with professional assistance when indicated. Individual approaches are essential, and not merely desirable. Always discuss and practise techniques with other adults; and have those that are significant in the child's life agree to a common approach before implementing with any children and, in particular, those with ASD. You will usually only have one chance to get it right, after which children will be deeply suspicious or experience anticipatory anxiety. Always seek additional advice and help, as children with ASD are particularly different from one another and typical children in their abilities and functioning. What works with one child may only ever work with that one child – and sometimes only for one day.

In ASD, the challenges faced by and with a child will not usually be resolved by tackling the visible issues directly. Indeed, the underlying difficulty may never be resolvable. The reason they may behave in a certain way may have a wide variety of causes and the relevant cause may have nothing to do with anything of which you may be aware.

Always explain to them what will occur, in advance, calmly and in simple short sentences. This is as important for children without speech, even if they are perceived to have limited understanding. For children with difficulties in communicating or understanding other people's communication, or with hearing or other difficulties, demonstrating on a toy or with simple drawings on paper or, for someone with vision impairment, with a finger on their hand, may also be helpful. 'No Surprises' is a rule that cannot be overstated. Others are: 'No Failures', that is, the next step for the child should be within their capability, erring on the side of caution; 'Keep It Calm' avoids adding to the distress; 'Keep It Simple', because complexity confuses and exacerbates anxiety; and 'Stay Positive'. This last refers to the actual communication *content* rather than style. Even in an emergency, tell *any* child what it is that you want them to do, clearly, rather than what you don't want them to do. For example, use 'walk with me' or 'stop where you are', rather than 'don't run'; or 'hands to sides' rather than 'don't hit'.

Words that are CAPITALISED are cross references to topics that are listed in the contents and described in more detail elsewhere in the book.

Autism Spectrum Disorder including Asperger's (ASD for short)

(Asperger's Syndrome and autism are classified under the umbrella term of Autism Spectrum Disorders or ASD, according to the *Diagnostic and Statistical Manual of Mental Disorders, DSM-5*.[1,2])

Autism is typically agreed to be a condition that is present at birth and known as a neuro-developmental disability. It is a condition that is present in and affects some people's brains. It causes differences in the way people with ASD grow and mature mentally in most areas controlled by the thinking, communicating, emoting and, as a result, the behaving parts of their brain. It is a broad description or 'spectrum' condition with great diversity in the presentation, abilities and difficulties of people who have it. The diagnosis indicates various difficulties in typical life development across different areas of functioning.

For a formal diagnosis of ASD, there are mainly two features, described later in this section. Problematically, helping someone with ASD is too often seen as simplistically 'fixing' these problems. For example, sensory sensitivities are sometimes treated with desensitising by using brushes on children's arms and other simple techniques; or with 'integration' therapy, even if there is no scientific evidence for this (and there is none in this case according to the American Academy of Paediatrics) and it causes increased anxiety and the suppression of natural aversive reactions or has no benefit at all.[3] Another common difficulty in ASD is with handwriting, often described as a fine motor skill difficulty. For decades, children have been required to do wrist-strengthening exercises, usually with bands and weights, though there has never been any evidence of beneficial effects. This problem seems to really be in the brain, where the language centres have difficulty in communicating with the motor centres (this is a very simplified explanation).

The first diagnostic criterion in the DSM-5 is that people with autism have difficulties in social communication and interactions with others. These are seen as differences in spoken communication (see SPEECH, LANGUAGE) and SOCIAL SKILLS behaviour. Some children and adults with ASD may have no speech at all. Some people with ASD may have the ability to speak but only do so to certain people, as in SELECTIVE MUTISM. Others may have long, complex, even pressured speech, sometimes earning the label 'little professors'. In social situations, they usually have some challenges, from manageable anxiety through to phobia or behaving quite inappropriately.

Social skills training has simplistically been seen as an ASD panacea treatment or fix, with many programmes focusing exclusively on these skills.

While learning a form of communication is a major asset, language may prove impossible and is not essential. Social skills are typically poorly translated from each age and developmental stage to the next, and from a skills training programme to any real-life situation. Appropriate behaviours can be 'drilled' to replace those that are inappropriate, but nuanced or subtle selection of the correct behaviour for a context is unlikely to develop beyond natural ability. Parents who behave in certain ways, such as commenting on other people, using idioms or swearing at home, should not be critical of their children for doing so at school or in public. Adults may need to admit that the child with ASD may have much better recall of what was said than they do. A child with ASD approaching a stranger and commenting critically on their appearance after having heard another person do so is one of those real-life nightmares for parents. Children with ASD continue to develop all their skills on their individual trajectory, as do typical children, until in their mid- to late twenties, and this is also true of social behaviour, so some rough edges polish off as they age and acquire additional social attributes.

The second aspect for formal diagnosis is behaviour or interests or thoughts that are unusual in being restricted or repetitive. This can include repetitive actions such as rocking, or sorting blocks into colours, or watching the same or similar videos repeatedly. In adults it may be in preferring to do highly structured and/or repetitive work; for example, computer coding, book-keeping or working in narrow areas of academia or law. Not everyone who does such work, though, has autism.

Correcting these repetitive behaviours by enforced regulation, such as stopping a child from fidgeting, may exacerbate their anxiety so they are quite unable to concentrate and learn. Enforced curtailment may also result in far less acceptable behaviours. As an experiment, *only with an adult you know extremely well,* when they are jiggling or twitching while simultaneously talking or undertaking some other complex but not dangerous activity (for example, not while they are driving), stop their repetitive behaviour by placing your hand to stop or draw attention to the offending action. Inevitably, they will lose concentration and stop talking or the other parallel activity. For some people, and not only those with ASD, perseveratively talking may be the repetitive activity that allows them to manage complex situations. Stopping them from talking may cause them visible distress. So how can this be managed in a classroom so as not to disturb other children?

Again, simplistic approaches to treatment with desensitisation, behaviour modification and even distracting or diverting are unlikely to bring about desired improvements.

Somewhat oddly, under this second major element of the formal diagnosis is included: 'hyper- or hyporeactivity to sensory input or unusual interests in sensory aspects of the environment', including indifference or over-sensitivity to pain, temperature, specific sounds or textures, as well as excessive smelling or touching of objects, visual fascination with lights or movement, such as fans or wheels. There are also many other elements to autism that are not captured in the formal diagnosis and as many as possible of these are covered in this book.

The term Asperger's Syndrome was often used to describe someone with high functioning autism. Officially this term was removed from the diagnostic manual in 2013,[4] but some people prefer to continue to use the term for themselves or just use the word 'Aspie'. A warning: some people with ASD truly dislike this term. Some prefer the term 'autistic', but these are very personal decisions. Most truly dislike being called 'an autistic', as if the condition was their only attribute. Different abilities in people with ASD are common and may include incredible memory, sharp vision, acute hearing and sometimes mathematical skills, for example (see SENSORY SENSITIVITIES). Others, such as Stephen Wiltshire, an ASD hero, are incredible artists, and in his case also having an eidetic or photographic memory for cityscapes.[5] On the other hand, ordinary ASD and typical attributes and difficulties are much more common than these unusual abilities. Let's face it, we are all for the most part quite average in each of our own unique ways.

For the diagnosis, some delays in different areas of thinking, language and behaviour, including social skills and functioning, will be present. The delays may be much more noticeable and create greater difficulties in some children than others. Unfortunately, hidden impairments, those not obvious, may not receive attention and become increasingly problematic.

Differences in children with ASD are usually recognised between the ages of 12 and 24 months,[6,7,8] although this can be earlier if the delays are more obvious. People with high functioning autism (previously Asperger's Syndrome) may at times not receive a diagnosis until they are much older. Indeed, they can experience lifelong difficulties with no recognition or support and inappropriate attention, and even medical interventions with medication and involuntary treatments. The challenges associated with ASD can be just as difficult and stressful for the people with ASD and their families, particularly when it comes to daily social interactions and life skills.[9]

A

Animals

Pets have been found to be effective in assisting in reducing anxiety in some children with autism and sometimes even with their social skill development. Research supports the idea that children with autism can experience benefits from interacting with pets, for the most part in the direct reduction of anxiety.[10] As many children with ASD experience significant stress and anxiety in their daily lives, pets can offer comfort and make a positive contribution to their social and emotional development.[11] This is not always the case, however, and some children have become abjectly distressed at the introduction of an animal into their home.

Animal-assisted therapies can provide ways to teach appropriate behaviour as well as assist in increasing children's communication skills, moderating behaviour and social integration. This should not be overstated. A pet is not a solution to every problem. Children with ASD usually have difficulty in taking information learned in one situation and applying it appropriately in another. The child may not be able to care for the animal, placing an additional burden on an already stretched family, and may cause problems through its introduction. A cautious approach is best.

There are specially trained and quite expensive Autism Assistance Dogs, who have the same legal rights of access as Guide Dogs for people with visual impairment.[12] They are usually used with children and some adults with severe difficulties arising from their ASD. Families and children undergo weeks of training with their dog. Often these dogs are attached to the child's belt by a lead, and they will sit or lie down if the child is moving into a dangerous situation.

Anxiety (see also Fight-flight)

People with ASD often worry about many things in their everyday life, many more and much more deeply than typical people. The world can be a very surprising, confusing and complex place for children (and adults) with ASD. They may have a lot of trouble coping with unfamiliar social or other situations (see SOCIAL STORIES™). Their difficulties with understanding what others may be thinking, feeling or how they may react can make them think that people and situations are unpredictable and overwhelming. A child may struggle to recognise their anxiety and know how to communicate this. Instead, they may behave in ways that cause them, their peers and you great distress. These behaviours may be called challenging, oppositional, defiant or even naughty. Usually it is a distress reaction, although if not treated early it can deteriorate. Visible signs of anxiety include:

- insisting on routine and sameness; a common trait of ASD

- difficulty shifting between tasks, thoughts and emotions, or doing so rapidly (see TRANSITIONS)

- SLEEP difficulties; whether going to sleep, staying asleep, or early or late waking

- FOOD fussiness; taste, texture, colours, temperature or even utensils such as plates and cutlery

- MELTDOWNS may be explosive or silent, withdrawal, rocking, head banging

- social withdrawal; for example, hiding in their room at their birthday party (see SOCIAL SKILLS)

- BOLTING, which may be a direct flight response

- obsessions and rituals (see ROUTINES, OCD)

- so-called self-stimulatory behaviour (stimming), which may really be calming behaviours; flapping, spinning, pacing or rocking (see STEREOTYPIES)

- self-harm; hair pulling, skin scratching, nail biting, head banging, biting their skin, cutting, burning, puncturing (see HARM, PAIN, SENSORY SENSITIVITIES).

Remember that these are survival behaviours and attempting to understand them, rather than label them negatively, for example, as naughty, oppositional or disobedient, will in the long term be far more helpful to children and their families.

There is also an unusual and not well known or understood aspect of ASD. Children with ASD have *dis*similar cortisol peak times and rates of production compared with typical children.[13] Most people experience a doubling of their cortisol levels on waking, which allows them to prepare for their day. As commented upon in SLEEP, elevated cortisol at night detrimentally affects sleep. Typical children also exhibit aroused levels at times of changing activities, perhaps facilitating the additional mental effort required to undertake change.[14]

It usually takes assistance from a paediatric mental health professional, such as a clinical psychologist, to properly help children overcome anxiety (see PROFESSIONALS).

Applied Behaviour Analysis (ABA)
(see also Early intervention, EIBI)

Mostly associated with the work of Ole Ivar Løvaas conducted over half a century, ABA is a standardised teaching intervention based on behavioural, also known as Classical, learning principles.[15] The approach arose from his ground-breaking research and clinical practice aimed at improving the lives of families that have children with autism. In 1965, he explained his approach for organising the recording of observed behaviours. He described an innovative study of triggers and consequences that precipitate, maintain and exacerbate challenging behaviours. He further developed these methods to a comprehensive approach of teaching children who were unable to speak, to do so. In his articles, Løvaas also described how to use social reinforcers (rewards), how to teach children to imitate social behaviour and how to reduce life-threatening self-injury and aggression. After a follow-up of his interventions (in 1973), he and his colleagues proposed several additional ways to improve outcomes such as commencing intervention during children's preschool years instead of later in childhood or adolescence, as well as involving parents and implementing the intervention in the family's home.

ABA came to be added to behaviour modification (see BEHAVIOUR). From previously only trying to alter problematic behaviour, behaviour analysts try to understand the function of that behaviour, what antecedents (triggers) promote the behaviour and what reinforcers maintain it and how it can be replaced by successful behaviour. The analysis is based on careful observations and assessment of a function of behaviour and the testing of strategies that produce measurable changes. ABA remains one of the most widely used, robust and successful of interventions for children with ASD and a precursor to implementing behaviour modification.

ABA is incorporated into other early interventions.

Often when reading about it, you may encounter the term 'Contemporary ABA'. This has arisen as the original form of ABA included some punitive elements (punishments), which have been largely removed for being ineffective.

Assessments

To be diagnosed with ASD, your child will need a comprehensive diagnostic assessment and interviews with a professional health specialist such as a paediatrician or a clinical psychologist with particular training in the diagnosis of ASD (see PROFESSIONALS). While the paediatrician is the expert on the physical nature of disorder, they will usually refer to a clinical psychologist who is an expert in the cognitive and behavioural aspects of ASD. Following the assessment, the clinical psychologist should provide a set of strategies to assist with difficult behaviours and teaching techniques.

For many educational departments, even if a comprehensive assessment is made that arrives at the diagnosis, this will need to be 'verified' by a paediatrician, psychiatrist or neurologist. On occasion, the medical professional may choose to prescribe medication before providing confirmation, or even refusing to do so. This can be costly to parents and an imposition on the child. There is no medicine to treat autism and there are no Cochrane Reviews indicating the benefit of medication for ASD. (The *Cochrane Database of Systematic Reviews* is the leading resource for systematic reviews in health care.[16])

For some parents, the assessment process can be stressful, confusing and even upsetting. Health professionals understand that the diagnosis can have a big impact on parents and families so they will answer any questions you may have. They may seek to discuss this with school personnel and the child's teachers.

The assessment process carefully evaluates your child's social behaviour and speech skills, strengths and weaknesses. It should also formally assess your child's cognitive functioning or how they think. The assessment can take some time as the health professional will gather all this information through interviews with you and your child's school teachers. In some cases, the health professional may even ask to observe your child in natural settings, such as at school or at home. Once they have gathered all the information they need to make a diagnosis; the health professional will provide you with feedback and recommendations for strategies, support and services that will best meet your child's individual needs. They may also involve paediatricians, speech and occupational therapists and other professionals (see PROFESSIONALS).

An assessment conducted by a paediatrician or clinical psychologist will usually include the following components, although they may be conducted by different people over different consultations:[17]

- Information about the family history, including of the parents, uncles and aunts, nieces and nephews and grandparents.

- A formal interview about the child's perinatal and developmental history.

- A neuro-cognitive assessment to understand how the child's brain thinks; depending on indications, this is likely to include an assessment of the child's INTELLIGENCE AND IQ, EXECUTIVE FUNCTION, MEMORY, LEARNING (ability and approach) and, for school-age children, assessment of their academic abilities.

- It may include the conduct of the Autism Diagnostic Observation Schedule (ADOS), an assessment of communication, social interaction and play, the Autism Diagnostic Interview – Revised (ADI-R) or the Diagnostic Interview for Social and Communication Disorders (DISCO).

- It may also include a number of questionnaires to be answered by parents and teachers, and consultations with the child and their parents or carers.

- If not recently conducted, a medical assessment may also be advised, including a comprehensive physical examination and history with hearing and vision tests, blood tests, an electroencephalogram (EEG) and, less frequently, genetic testing and testing for lead.

Attention Deficit Hyperactivity Disorder (ADHD)

ADHD is a neuro-developmental mental disorder with problems of attending (concentrating) or attention (direction), excessive activity (agitation) or difficulty controlling behaviour which may not be age-appropriate (for example, only being able to attend while dancing or pacing).

In children, problems paying attention may result in poor school performance. It is extremely common as COMORBIDITY, thought to be present in between 25 per cent and 40 per cent of people with ASD,[18] although no research is apparent. Symptoms typically begin by the age of six and, for a diagnosis, should persist for more than six months.[19] Although it causes impairment, particularly in modern society, many children with ADHD may have good attention for tasks on which they are helped to focus or which they find interesting. In Australia, the ADHD diagnosis does not attract much school support, and often the first-line behavioural treatment recommended in most other countries is effectively secondary to the prescription of psycho-stimulants.

Both ADHD and ASD involve the EXECUTIVE FUNCTION or orbito-frontal part of the brain. This is also thought to be the centre for working MEMORY. As a result, indications in IQ assessments of deficits in working memory may indicate ASD, ADHD or comorbidity of both. Depending on the meeting of diagnostic criteria, one or other or both may be formally diagnosed. This should not affect the attention to, treatment of, or tailored teaching necessary for the child's optimum functioning.

There are three recognised types or presentations, but because symptoms can change over time, the presentation may change over time as well:

- *Combined:* if the required number of symptoms of both the criteria of inattention and hyperactivity–impulsivity were present for the past six months.

- *Predominantly Inattentive:* if the required number of symptoms of inattention, but not hyperactivity–impulsivity, were present for the past six months.

- *Predominantly Hyperactive–Impulsive:* if the required number of symptoms of hyperactivity–impulsivity, but not inattention, were present for the past six months.

ADHD is diagnosed approximately three times more frequently in boys than in girls. It can be difficult to tell apart from some other disorders such as ASD, as well as just from everyday exuberance or energetic activities that are still within the normal range.

ADHD management recommendations vary by country and usually involve some combination of behavioural therapy, lifestyle changes, changes in the home and school environments and, in most countries as a last resort, medications. Medication is only recommended as an initial treatment in children who have severe symptoms and only usually after therapy has failed, although, in practice, medication is often used as co-therapy and quite often medication is trialled before other therapy. Stimulant medication therapy is not usually recommended as an initial therapy in preschool children. Adolescents and adults tend to progressively develop coping skills which can remedy some or all of their ADHD-related behaviour. They may, however, still benefit from medication to assist with concentration.

There is no evidence that stimulant medication improves academic ability or IQ, although it is often sought to do so by university students and some parents.

Awareness and self-awareness – see Insight

B

Behaviour

Your child can behave in ways you may find difficult or a challenge to manage. They may:

- have trouble following instructions, perhaps not UNDERSTANDING or seeming to ignoring them

- behave in socially inappropriate ways such as taking their clothes off in public or directing impolite gestures or comments to other people (see SOCIAL SKILLS)

- be aggressive to others, including their siblings, peers, teachers and other family members (HARM)

- have trouble calming themselves when they have MELTDOWNS (see CALM, BREATHING)

- engage in self-stimulatory (calming) behaviour such as hand-flapping, rocking or tapping (see ROUTINES, STEREOTYPIES)

- hurt themselves or other children such as biting, scratching, hitting or head banging (see PAIN).

Children with ASD can behave in challenging ways because they may be feeling worried or anxious. This could be because they have trouble understanding what is going on around them, including interpreting what other people are communicating through their words, facial expressions or body language. There may also be non-human triggers such as bright light, heat, noise or just an overwhelming cluster of different events. Your child may struggle to communicate with you, causing them and you significant distress and frustration. They may perceive almost anything as potentially threatening and so a No Surprises and Keep It Calm policy can work wonders.

The first step to managing your child's challenging behaviours is for *you* to stay CALM. Where possible, try to identify the triggers. For example, your child may become very upset, even at being asked, 'How was school?' This can be an inordinately difficult question for a child with ASD to answer (see FLUID REASONING). They may simply not understand the question. Following a recent family tragedy, a highly intelligent adult was asked, 'How are you coping?' His response: 'As I am.' Understanding how we are feeling can be difficult for any of us. If we are literal, this may require an instant review of our entire body and mind. If we have working MEMORY difficulties, we may not be able to conclude this without forgetting bits as well as the original question.

A child with ASD exhibiting challenging behaviour may be distressed when there has been a change to their usual routine, perhaps at home or from school. They may have a particular 'ritual' they must complete before moving on to another activity. Many more possible triggers and some solutions are included under their respective letter of the alphabet.

Self-stimulatory (stimming), repetitive and perseverative behaviours are all slightly different in their meaning, but may all have the same trigger and cause (see STEREOTYPIES). The cause seems to have much to do with the EXECUTIVE FUNCTION area of the brain which may prolong activities and have difficulty in initiating new ones. Some children may find that the calm feeling associated with repetition reduces anxiety. Anything that appears to intrude on the persisting behaviour, even the need to go to bed, may cause deep anxiety.

The most effective treatments are described under EARLY INTERVENTION and TOKEN REWARD SYSTEMS, but these can also be effectively introduced at later stages of development. The earlier, however, the better. *Caution:* Introduce the intervention as an entire and properly developed approach. Failures in the introduction of interventions are difficult to remedy as they can become triggers to additional distress.

Bolting

Many children with ASD bolt when they are distressed or distracted. First, like all children, children with ASD may see something of interest and wander or run off to see it closer. This is not unusual or necessarily a sign of ASD. Quite often, this may be an item of typical interest to that child and may be a train set, Lego, a spinning fan, an animal or another child.

There is also the quite common flight response as a result of ANXIETY. The fight and flight (and less so freeze) responses (see also FIGHT-FLIGHT) are our natural defences to threat, and children with ASD, and for that matter everyone else, may perceive a threat where there is none. They may actively misinterpret behaviour or events in such a way as to see it as a threat. Woe betide people who unsuspectingly try to touch some children and adults with ASD. It is quite common for children (and some adults) with ASD with SENSORY SENSITIVITIES, or just a fear of how the touch may progress, to immediately lash out.

In other cases, children may perceive a situation as threatening because of sensory stimuli and wish to escape them or they may perceive a situation in unexpected ways or react like Clint, described in IMPULSIVITY, where he punched his grandfather a year after seeing him as a result of remembering that he smoked, and Clint did not like the smell.

Many strategies may be necessary for 'bolting'. If the child is likely to dart off anywhere, then close attention, or in extreme cases a lead, may be necessary; particularly for small children who may run across a road. For children who frequently do so in certain known situations, practise the 'bolting' strategy with the child by calmly talking them through the situation. 'When the aeroplane flies overhead, this is what you can do.' This may include putting on headphones or ear muffs, walking to their room, listening to music, going to a particular part of the garden, and so on. An important element may be signalling that they know what they are doing and are alright. As they walk or run off, they give a 'thumbs up' or 'high-five' to a nearby responsible adult. This shows that they are following their bolting plan. Autism assistant dogs can be most helpful with serious bolting behaviours (see ANIMALS).

Breathing

Breathing is often thought of as a technique for reducing anxiety in children. While it can be helpful, it can also cause additional anxiety. It needs to be taught in each situation where your child experiences anxiety such as home or school, but only when they are CALM. Teaching it in any artificial situation, such as a clinic, is unlikely to be as helpful. We know that children with ASD have difficulty in generalising.

The technique is really important, and telling children with ASD to take a deep breath is most unhelpful. Just think about what happens when you experience a sudden fright. Typically, we all take a quick deep breath. This is both preparation for FIGHT–FLIGHT and a signal to our body to arm all of our defence systems for whatever threat may be coming. When this happens, our rather marvellous sympathetic nervous system, which ensures our survival, kicks in. This includes fighting, fleeing and freezing, depending on us and the situation. It also is anything but being relaxed. It can cause children to panic. So, deep breathing is out.[20]

Best approaches with children are 'sleepy time' (pretend sleep) or 'tidal' (tide in, tide out) breathing. Both are slow breaths in, pauses, slow breaths out and pause again. This is about slow and gentle breathing and not about holding breaths. Remember that children tend to breathe more rapidly than adults anyway and that what may be a comfortable relaxing count of 1, 2, 3, 4, for an adult, may be a breathless and terrifying eternity for a child. For example, children from one to four years of age breathe 20 to 40 times per minute while resting.[21] There is an increasing practice of using horses to help children with ASD control anxiety by breathing at the same rate. However, horses' respiratory rate is half that of children,[22] so such techniques can actually exacerbate rather than improve anxiety in some children.

When teaching children about breathing, be really careful about the set-up. Practise in a quiet place. The child may prefer to do it with a favourite toy or comforter. Let them look at a blank wall or natural scene with no distractions with their eyes open. Sit next to them rather than opposite them. Tell them that if they feel like closing their eyes they can do so at any time. You will stay with them and nothing will change. They can also open their eyes at any time, but suggest in advance they do so slowly – to avoid dizziness.

Bullying

Unfortunately, bullying exists in life and work and is commonly seen in school settings. It can take many forms and can sometimes be difficult to recognise. It can be physical, verbal or through social media. It may also be inconsistent in that calling a big strong football player 'shorty' or 'skinny' can be an appreciated term of affection, but used on a slightly built child it can cause distress. Children who are different, including those with ASD, are often a target for bullies. As people with ASD struggle with social understanding and communication, they can be susceptible to bullying and social exclusion.

Children with ASD do not understand these social nuances and so may perceive friendliness as bullying or be perceived as a bully when they call a smaller child names, repeating what they may have heard other children exchange as banter between them. Bullying usually involves one or more people repeatedly, and usually intentionally, using hurtful words or actions; but people with ASD may use the words unintentionally and still cause hurt to others.

They may even perceive bullying as friendship or 'cool' and engage in deliberate bullying themselves. They may also misperceive friendship as bullying. It's really confusing for them. Your child may not realise that they are being bullied or rejected. You may notice that your child appears distressed (see ANXIETY), upset or angry, have injuries such as bruises or scratches, torn clothing or missing items. You may even notice an increase in challenging behaviours, nightmares, poor sleep or your child refusing (see REFUSAL) to go to school. Bullying can have a profoundly negative impact on your child's social and emotional wellbeing so it is important that you, your child and school teachers are aware of this and seek support as early as possible. If you are concerned that your child may be being bullied at school, be calm and direct in asking your child if anyone has made them sad. Do seek professional assistance as early as possible as this can become a major influence in your child's life.

If you have concerns, raise them with the school, even if you are unsure. Expect positive indications that they are following up your concerns with greater attention to your child. Most schools and education systems have anti-bullying policies and will state them to you. Children at school are still children and will do what they have always done notwithstanding rules and regulations. If necessary, ask to have your child observed at play.

You can effectively use strategies such as SOCIAL STORIES™ 23 to explain appropriate and inappropriate behaviour to your child for both how they should behave to others and how others should behave towards them. If your child shows unexplained distress, then 'Comic Strip Conversations'24 can be helpful in disentangling the cause. Both approaches are found detailed in books by Carol Gray.

C

Calm

For any home, this is a worthwhile goal and not always possible. For a family with a child with ASD, it is almost *the* most important goal for everyone. Building on the idea of No Surprises, everyone learning to be and stay calm can make a significant difference. Just one example can be the benefit to everyone of the whole family waking up 15 minutes earlier in the morning to ensure chores can be completed without stress. Any extra time can be used to sit quietly as a family or do some simple activity such as throwing a ball. Most families report that when they develop this routine, they seem to have much more time in their day and enjoy all aspects of their life much more. Just think how much time could be saved if there were not daily upsets first thing in the morning.

Care

Obviously parents should and do care for their children (see PARENTING). What parents may forget to do, however, is care for themselves. While this is important for all parents, it is utterly essential for parents of children with disabilities. Children with ASD can be most challenging, every day, with little respite from the intensity of their interpersonal interactions. Meeting their needs, and if you have to do this without support, can be so exhausting as to make some parents physically ill. Your mental and physical health are most important. To look after yourself, it is important to keep active in enjoyable ways. You may want to exercise, study or work, or just have fun. There are parents of children with ASD everywhere and, as a result, there are many and varied support groups.

Participating in such a group can be most helpful. Interacting with people where the subject of conversation can be different is also important. This can be an entirely social group or a similar interests group with nothing to do with ASD. You may need holidays and even days off. You may need a night to go out and have some fun. You are absolutely entitled to have as much of a life as anyone else. If you are unable to access services to assist you in achieving balance in your life, speak to one of the health professionals helping your child. They should all be able to assist you to find support services, including respite care on either a casual or regular basis.

Celebration

There will be many challenges in parenting children with ASD and for the children themselves. Even small achievements need to be celebrated. Simply, this may be a 'high-five', three cheers, a celebratory dance, a special treat of a minor nature or your family's special recognition of achievement. Other items that can be particularly relished are, for example, a cupcake – and don't forget the sparkler and a home-made printed certificate for having sat still or calmly during a difficult period, to be presented in front of the whole family, including pets, and hung on the wall as a reminder. Think of how many celebrations you can invent to recognise your child's achievements; and do not forget to recognise your own.

Clothes

Clothes are very important to people with ASD. Due to their sensory issues, certain types and textures of clothing can feel very uncomfortable and distressing. They may not like how certain materials feel against their skin or are sensitive to the itchy sensation of clothing labels. Some may even like to wear lots of clothes on a hot day or feel upset with sensations such as wet clothes that stick to their body. When you buy clothing for your child, be sure that they can try it on to check to see whether they are comfortable with it. *Hint:* Remove labels as they can be prickly even to people not on the spectrum. Clothes can be an important element of any child's IDENTITY, and particularly so in ASD. One child refused to attend school as he was not allowed to wear a 'Super Mario' T-shirt. When this was understood, the solution was found in having him wear it under his school shirt.

For children with GENDER dysphoria, this can be distressing to the point of self-harm. Different strategies may be needed for every child. If just dressing as they choose is not possible for whatever reasons, sports clothes or shorts under skirts may work for a transgender boy while wearing dresses at home may be part of the solution for a transgender girl. Forcing children to conform against their deep wishes can be seriously injurious to their mental wellbeing and affect them for the rest of their lives. Creativity and sensitivity can be applied as much to clothing as other challenging areas.

Cognitive Behavioural Therapy – see Therapies

Communication

Speaking effectively with other people can be particularly challenging for many people with ASD. Speech is not essential, however, and many people learn to communicate in other ways. Some are able to develop language and communication skills, others may struggle significantly and some may not have any language at all. For many parents, this can be very stressful and frustrating as this can make everything more challenging when it comes to providing instructions, teaching and managing behaviour. Often people with ASD do not understand that communication is a two-way process and that it involves the use of both listening and speech and gestures that include words, eye contact, facial expressions and behaviours. For example, kicking a ball back to someone is a friendly communication (see LANGUAGE, SPEECH and HEARING).

Despite the communication difficulties your child may be experiencing, most can be helped to develop their abilities in communication skills of different types over time and they will benefit from your help. If your child has significant difficulties with speech, language and other non-verbal communication skills, it may be helpful to consult with a paediatrician, clinical psychologist, speech pathologist or special education teacher at school. It is important to help your child develop effective communication skills that suit their ability as it will improve their development and life skills, and their enjoyment of life as well as their learning and behaviour. Most children can be helped to achieve some level of direct (non-interpreted) communication and should continually be encouraged to do so. You never know when your child may achieve the ability, become sufficiently confident or overcome their anxiety to communicate. (See also Mikey's story under SELECTIVE MUTISM.)

Comorbidity

Comorbidity refers to the presence of one or more additional disorders that occur with a primary disorder. Research has found that many people with autism are more likely to have related conditions, which can complicate treatment and lead to more challenging behaviours. Some commonly associated conditions found in people with autism include: Attention Deficit Hyperactivity Disorder (ADHD), Obsessive Compulsive Disorder (OCD), bipolar disorder, depression, Generalised Anxiety Disorder (GAD), intellectual disability, Tourette's Syndrome, other tic disorders, seizures and epilepsy, as well as sensory, visual and gastrointestinal problems and gender dysphoria and body dysmorphia. Children with ASD are more likely to experience symptoms of ADHD, whereas depression is commonly seen in adolescents and adults. If your child experiences any of these other conditions, it can be helpful to use a multidisciplinary approach involving a team of health PROFESSIONALS such as paediatricians, clinical psychologists, speech pathologists, physiotherapists and occupational therapists to support your child's individual needs.

Creativity and conceptual blindness

In order to make sense of our world, our brains need to look at the context in which the information is presented for us to understand what this actually means. For example, when we try to get a sense of what someone is communicating to us, we look at how they communicate by interpreting their words, facial expressions, body language, the tone of their voice and the environment we are in, when this occurs. People may be telling us something of which we have no experience, perhaps an overseas trip. Our imagination, abstract ability, creativity and FLUID REASONING may help us fill in the blanks. People with ASD are usually great on factual detail but may struggle to imagine something outside their direct experience as well as the context or the bigger picture. This may contribute to their difficulty in understanding communication or ideas in ways that make sense to people with typical brains. As people with ASD are literal ('raining cats and dogs' means animals falling from the sky) and dichotomous (black/white, right/wrong) thinkers, it can be hard for them to think abstractly or from different perspectives (see THEORY OF MIND, UNDERSTANDING, fluid reasoning). These concepts are easily and usually intuitive without conscious effort, grasped by most typical people.

Many people with ASD struggle with abstract creativity and imagination, which can make it hard for them to imagine what a particular idea or experience may be without actually having gone through the experience themselves. As people with ASD develop and have more life experience, this difficulty remains but can be less obvious. For children, it can be particularly difficult and anxiety-provoking. Many people with ASD may be thought of as creative and the author's favourite, Stephen Wiltshire, is certainly so in a particular sense. He draws cityscapes he sees, with great accuracy and detail, almost as a living camera with the human advantage of binocular vision and human imprecision which all combine to make his art such a delight to so many. At the same time, his website shows no purely abstract creative renderings. Similarly, a brilliant technical musician with ASD may be quite unable to vary their playing of a particular piece of music as they may feel there can only be one correct way to do so.

D

Death

Understanding the concept of death can be scary, confusing and overwhelming for many if not most children and adults. Those with autism may have more difficulty understanding death, for many reasons. The idea of death and its reality may be beyond their ability to grasp. Death often leads to unexpected or overwhelming emotions or behaviours from other adults and children who have been affected by the death. While the death itself may not cause an expected or common grief reaction in a person with ASD, the behaviours of the family may be distressing, and even if not directly so, their distress may be discerned and not understood. As children with autism have difficulty anticipating how things may be after the death of someone, it is important for parents and families to have a thorough discussion of this topic so as to better prepare them for the future. For adults with religious beliefs, as difficult as this may be, it should be kept as factual as possible to avoid confusion and perhaps inappropriate responses. People with ASD are very routine-oriented and therefore the unexpected death of someone can be seen as a disruption to their usual routine.

Not only can this cause significant distress to them, it can also be very difficult for them to comprehend what has happened and understand that this could negatively affect other people involved. The person with ASD's reaction or lack of reaction may also be distressing to others.

Another aspect is that children with ASD may be shockingly matter-of-fact about death or not understand it to the point of ignoring it. One child approached a religious minister at a funeral to ask how long it would take the worms to eat the body and pursued it to ask if worms might become ill as a result of the person having had cancer. Another giggled through a memorial service because everything looked and sounded so strange. Afterwards when, belatedly, the situation was explained, he became distraught at the event and his behaviour. Anticipating and explaining factually can make a world of difference around complex subjects such as birth, illness and death.

Decisions (see also Fluid reasoning)

Children and most people with ASD have difficulty in making decisions. While the difficulty can vary in its intensity, from a complete inability to do so to some considerable skill in deductive reasoning, it appears to be at least partly the case for most with ASD. This can have implications for almost every area of life. The difficulty may reach its pinnacle in everyday, arbitrary decisions; how does one decide which pair of black socks to wear? For many ordinary decisions they may come down to a completely 'whimsical' choice based on some non-rational, possibly emotional, basis. Should we buy the can of the same brand of beans on the left or right?

Every moment of every day, we make these completely unimportant decisions without thinking. People with ASD may be unable to do so, looking for some logical basis without finding one and causing themselves significant and potentially disabling anxiety. The extent of the distress that this may cause cannot be sufficiently emphasised. It may be entirely disabling. It can relegate the person to living out their lives in one room wearing the same clothes and eating the same food, day in and day out. They may only watch one particular TV series or play one computer game. They may unconsciously 'decide', usually through progressive withdrawal, that this is the only solution to their irresolvable quandary of what to do with every element of their lives. Even though this may be the case, they may also lack INSIGHT into what is occurring and develop any number of psychosomatic or social reasons to explain their behaviour. It is emphasised that many people may experience the following examples as quite genuine illnesses. For some with ASD, however, having stomach ailments, limb pain, headaches and any other physical condition which gives them a reason to not have to make decisions may be symptomatic of anxiety-provoking, pathological (illness- or condition-related) indecisiveness.

One thing about this condition is that we know with some certainty that indecisiveness and ASD are related. The area of the brain most agreed to be involved in EXECUTIVE FUNCTION is the frontal lobe.[25] The area believed most often compromised in ASD is the area of the frontal lobe immediately above our eyes called the orbito-frontal region.

We know from people who have suffered a brain injury in this area, through accident or illness, that they may become quite unable to make decisions, needing assistance with everyday activities, sometimes while still able to undertake more complex activities, often work-related or closely directed by others.[26]

The solution to the difficulty described earlier with the beans or any other similar or identical items, is that someone else needs to provide the rule. One such rule may be 'always select the item at the front, on the top at left'. These rules work and can alleviate anxiety to an amazing extent and be life-changing for the sufferer.

It must be added that not everyone suffering from indecisiveness has ASD. There are many other causes including natural ability and depression, to name just two.

Defecating (involuntary, unintentional, voluntary, encopresis, faecal incontinence) (see also Toileting)

The terms involuntary and voluntary defecating, encopresis and faecal incontinence all usually refer to, as the *Diagnostic and Statistical Manual* of the APA somewhat cutely states, the 'repeated passage of faeces into inappropriate places (e.g. underwear or floor) whether voluntary or unintentional'. It is typically caused by constipation, reflexive (involuntary) or deliberate (voluntary, intentional) withholding of stool, including a number of physical, psychological (anxiety) or neurological disorders (Hirschsprung's Disease). It can also be the quite deliberate expression of stool in places known to cause personal pleasure or a response, disquiet or distress in others (see FAECAL SMEARING).

Now, retention may occur. It is the large intestine's or colon's (an organ in the digestive system) job to remove excess water from stool (faeces). If for some reason, and there may be many, the stool remains in the colon too long and too much water is removed then the stool becomes hard and becomes painful for the child to expel in an ordinary bowel movement. Most adults have experienced this at some time. It may be caused by many things, including many medications. The poor child may avoid toileting to avoid the anticipated painful experience. There are many, inter-related, physical mechanisms and psychological factors that facilitate normal continence (faecal expression). The distress from painful toileting may cause such a deep conditioning ('programming') of the natural holding response that a holding (retention, inhibitory) response results (formally called anismus). All hardened stool builds up and stretches the large intestine to the point where the child is no longer aware of the normal sensations of their bowel movements. Some softer stool will leak around the blockage and result in soiling. The child has no control over these accidents and may not even be aware that they have occurred. In most children, anxiety results from repeated attempts and failures to control embarrassing soiling. Usually increasing anxiety will complicate the use of common treatments including stool softeners and behavioural strategies.

The usual onset of involuntary soiling may be associated with toilet training, including demands of the child to sit for a long time on a potty or toilet until they are productive. Another may be intense negative reactions from parents to the toileting process, faeces or other related behaviour.

Commencing school or preschool without being toilet trained, or even just the experience of school with all its novelty, including open shared toilets, can be highly problematic. This can be exacerbated in conservative families where children may never have defecated in front of others, never seen others do so, or have received critical responses when they have defecated. Domestic violence, authoritarian adults, moving home and/or school, and divorce can also negatively impact toileting behaviours and promote constipation. The original cause may become less significant as chronic physical and psychological distress continues.

The medical approach usually involves cleaning out using a laxative, using stool-softening agents and then scheduling sitting times, typically after meals and at regular intervals. Parental and sibling behaviour around the sitting should be calm, supportive and quietly reinforcing of the desired behaviour of defecating appropriately and even of unproductive sitting. (See also TOKEN REWARD SYSTEMS.)

Depression

People with ASD are more likely to experience depression (Major Depressive Disorder), ANXIETY (Generalised Anxiety Disorder) and OBSESSIVE COMPULSIVE DISORDER (OCD) in adolescence and adulthood. This may occur in relation to their struggles with social relationships, interacting with others and being able to anticipate what might happen in certain situations. They may also have trouble with finding and maintaining a job, social isolation and problems adapting to a non-ASD or ASD-unfriendly world. There is also some research to indicate that there may be a difference in the 'wiring' of autistic brains that makes them experience life in different ways and perhaps in more extreme ways, so making them more vulnerable to these other difficulties. Another area is the way in which people with ASD experience their own emotions (see EMOTIONS AND REGULATION). Even extremely high functioning adults with ASD describe perceiving their emotions in only two ways: content or upset (unhappy, depressed, stressed, anxious or angry).

Children can experience depression from an early age. They may not recognise it for what it is, unlike typical children and adults, unless they have a perception of the slightly different nature of their feelings; such as stressed compared with irritable, for example. Children with ASD, and into adulthood, remain quite unable to differentiate between fine differences of emotions, and extensive efforts to help them to do this are seldom – if ever – fruitful. The best strategy is for them to learn when their 'contented' or 'okay' state is slipping, to avoid MELTDOWNS.

Children may even make statements about wanting to kill themselves. Stay calm! Very few children in the world ever do this, and there is no evidence for the relatively low rate of suicide (every suicide is a tragedy) in adults to include more people with ASD than other groups. They do, however, self-harm (see HARM), although usually quite carefully so as not to do serious injury. If you are concerned that your child may be experiencing depression, it is important to consult with a health professional who is experienced in ASD and understands how your child communicates. By helping your child communicate about their difficulties and develop strategies to improve their life, you can better understand them and help them by providing the support that they need. Remember that even when someone with ASD communicates about feelings, this may not be clear and they may not be able to clarify what it is that they are trying to communicate. Asking them lots of questions will likely only increase their distress. If you can, sit quietly and responsively with them, letting them know you are there to help. Statements such as 'When I can understand, I'll try to help' are more helpful than 'What's making you unhappy?'

Development

Children with ASD develop at a different rate compared with their typical peers. They may have better memories and an eye for detail and strengths not typically seen in other children. They may also be slower at developing their language, thinking and social skills. Some children with ASD may be slow to learn to walk, talk and sit up on their own. They may also have unusual GAIT; for example, toe-walking, posture, sitting with legs splayed and many other differences. You may notice that they are only able to say a few words or start to combine words and speak in short phrases when they are older than other children. In their early life, many children with ASD also tend to be slower at learning or have extremely narrow interests (see STEREOTYPIES). Development is a lifelong experience. In some areas, at times, children with ASD may be ahead of their peers and at other times fall behind. In many common areas of functioning and learning they are likely to be slightly behind their peers. As they move towards the senior years of school and transitioning to adulthood, one of the most challenging times of anyone's development, they may experience particular difficulties. Support and understanding should be sought with professional help.

Distress (see also Anxiety and Calm)

People with ASD can experience high levels of distress that may seem unusually intense or an overreaction. Sensory issues, anxiety and difficulties in communicating with others can be particularly stressful and difficult to resolve. Children with ASD experience greater intensity of emotional reaction compared with typical children and can have great difficulty regulating themselves and their emotions. This can often lead to increased distress, anger and frustration in their parents as it can be particularly challenging for you to reassure or calm your child. Children with ASD can experience extreme distress and anxiety when separating from parents or when their preconceived plans are not followed; or they may exhibit behavioural signs of their difficulty coping with change (see TRANSITIONS), in making mistakes or even when feeling as if they have failed at any attempted task.

E

Early intervention (EIBI)

This is important as after decades of research and helping children with autism, early and intensive behavioural approaches are the only interventions that have repeatedly been shown to help in improving the lives of children with autism. Understanding the terms and their differences and limitations will assist in navigating the minefield of therapies that may be offered to you and your child.

To the confusion of most parents, the following terms sound similar and may be used interchangeably by PROFESSIONALS. So first, here are some explanations of these as they may apply to the support your child receives. While the term 'early intervention' is often used informally by people who know little about the approach it embodies, it is shorthand for Early Intensive Behavioural Intervention (EIBI) and is used to help children with ASD[27,28] and other disabilities. The following is a list of typical elements:

- As implied, it begins at first diagnosis from the earliest possible, and even pre-mobile, stages of a child's development, but most preferably preschool.

- While it can be implemented later, it can require more time and over a longer period. It can be appropriate for any level of functioning to assist with behavioural needs. This can be helping with TOILETING or writing an essay.

- As recommended, it is intensive for some 25 to 40 hours per week and is conducted for two or more years.

- It is behavioural in that it encourages desired behaviour and discourages unwanted or inappropriate behaviour.

- Different strategies within the approach vary in how they modify behaviour and what behaviour they address.

- It is an intervention, that is, it is intended to change existing functioning.[29]

EIBI is the overarching model which includes APPLIED BEHAVIOUR ANALYSIS (ABA) and other related interventions (see THERAPIES).

The professional view of EIBI and ABA is worth quoting in full:

'The press for early identification comes from evidence gathered over the past 10 years that intensive early intervention in optimal educational settings results in improved outcomes in most young children with autism, including speech in 75% or more and significant increases in rates of developmental progress and intellectual performance... However, these kinds of outcomes have been documented only for children who receive 2 years or more of intensive intervention services during the preschool years...'[30]

This is part of the findings of a Consensus Panel including the American Academy of Neurology, American Academy of Family Physicians, American Academy of Paediatrics, American Psychological Association, Society for Developmental and Behavioural Paediatrics, and the National Institute of Child Health & Human Development.[31]

Applied Behaviour Analysis (ABA), as practised with children with ASD, uses scientifically based learning theory and systematically applies it to change behaviour. It may be used to increase desired behaviours such as self-feeding or studying or decreasing unwanted behaviours such as MELTDOWNS. The term is often used interchangeably with Early Intensive Behavioural Interventions (EIBI). Some confusion is that this is an approach used in many areas of scientific research. Therapeutic learning approaches for children using Early Intensive Behavioural Interventions (EIBI) include Applied Behaviour Analysis.

Some of the techniques used in ABA and EIBI are described below.

Functional Behaviour Assessment (FBA)

This term is used to describe different methods that allow researchers and practitioners to identify the reason why a specific behaviour is occurring. To undertake an effective FBA takes extensive training and is usually done by teams of multidisciplinary professionals:

- The assessment describes and defines what is called the target behaviour or the behaviour that is to be changed in detail, specifically and concretely. Generalisations such as 'always', 'sometimes' and 'usually' are to be avoided.

- It collects information to determine the possible functions of the target behaviour; for example, a meltdown may be reinforced by restraining which could provide sensory stimulation.

- It uses direct observation and indirect measures such as interviews and questionnaires as well as Functional analysis (see later).

- Following analysis of the data, it determines whether the behaviour is a result of a functional, skill or a performance (standard) deficit. Will a reinforcement strategy of desired behaviour (reward for sitting at the table) alone be sufficient or is some learning required (how to sit unsupported in a chair)?

- All the information is analysed in order to form a hypothesis (conjecture or presumed function of the behaviour).

- The chosen interventions are devised and tested. These should always be constructive. For example, stopping a child from running into a road may be by teaching them how to walk on a footpath, how to stand at an intersection, how to check for traffic or await an instruction. Correct trials should be reinforced. The wrong way would be to shout at them.

Functional analysis

Functional analysis as used in Functional Behaviour Assessment is the application of the principles of Operant Conditioning to establish the relationships between a trigger and the response.

Operant Conditioning is when a behaviour is changed (modified) through reinforcement. The term reinforcement includes both reward and punishment as both can modify behaviour. If a child is having a meltdown, the playing of music may help calm them; but on another occasion when they wish to listen to music, they may have a meltdown in order to do so.

Other techniques that may be used in EIBI are:

Discrete Trial Training (DTT)

This is a direct teaching approach based on Applied Behaviour Analysis (ABA) principles.[32] Sometimes itself referred to as 'ABA', DTT is only one of several strategies included under the umbrella terms of ABA and EIBI. Discrete Trial Training is a technique of breaking down necessary skill sets into small steps for managing day-to-day learning opportunities. By teaching small steps, a child can develop skills relatively more quickly before combining them to achieve more complex steps. A gradual, repetitive technique, usually DTT begins at a table and begins with preparation or 'readiness' skills such as sitting in a chair, progressing to attending (an important early step) while also decreasing distracting behaviours (self-stimulatory – see STEREOTYPIES) that may interfere with learning. These last should only be addressed where necessary to avoid distraction, as they can be calming behaviours. The term 'self-stimulatory' is a little confusing and 'self-engaging' may help in understanding why some children do this. The terms 'stimming' and 'stereotypy' are used to describe the same behaviours.

The child is reinforced for appropriate responses as frequently as they can be identified. In an ABA programme mixed and varied instructions from different programmes are included, of which DTT is one. A No Failures approach is used to teach skills so the child rapidly experiences success and competence and self-confidence in achieving skills independently.

Once new skills are achieved in a 'discrete' setting, generalisation needs to occur. Some children will be able to do so instinctively, while most others need systematic scheduling for generalisation. Learning occurs through having multiple examples demonstrated. Therapists are trained on how to deliver mixed programmes of different approaches to avoid rote and increase functional learning.

Verbal behaviour

This uses a functional account of language and was originally suggested by Skinner in 1957.[33] It is, confusingly, any behaviour where the cause is affected by the behaviour of another person. It teaches children to use language and communication in a functional context and uses their natural inclination to repeat or parrot what they have heard (see HEARING, SPEECH), to meet their needs or demands, comment on experiences and respond to questions of a conversational rather than functional nature.

This encourages learning as well as retention and better generalisation of skills.

Skinner's VB model includes:

- *Echoic:* repeating of sounds, blends, words and sentences.

- *Mand (from 'demand'):* learning the technique of requesting items, action or information.

- *Tact (from 'contact'):* comment on direct experience of what the child can hear, see, feel, taste or smell.

- *Intraverbal:* responding to conversational questions.

Verbal behaviour does not need to be vocal. For example, children may use PECS (Picture Exchange Communication System), Auslan,[34] BSL, ASL (all sign languages of deaf communities) or technology to effectively communicate with their peers and parents.

Natural Environment Training (NET)

This, simply, is helping your child to develop functional everyday skills in their environment where they interact with people and objects.[35] It is a natural extension of DTT and includes school, home and any other regular place they attend, including restaurants and church. Balance between NET and DTT is essential for a child to develop confidence in interacting in social (see SOCIAL SKILLS) settings. The natural environment is where your child needs to learn to apply appropriate communication skills (for example, only toileting where it is appropriate to do so). The goal is to teach your child the necessary skills to independently interact with others in these environments and to become self-motivated in their learning of new skills in different contexts. It is an approach to teaching social learning. As the dynamism of the natural environment seldom allows multiple opportunities for a child to experience particular events, training should be ongoing. Where possible, such as with close family, parents can arrange for the environment to present the learning situation more frequently, facilitating more learning opportunities. For an effective EIBI programme of skill development a good balance between providing NET and DTT components is essential.

Fluency

Fluency is a term used in EIBI and ABA to describe programmes that teach a child to become fluent in a particular skill. When they achieve fluency, it indicates they can use the skills effortlessly and without having to think. Each skill learned can then be used as a platform to learn other, more advanced, skills.

One strategy easily learned by all parents is to use simple language (short simple phrases) to describe everyday objects, activities and people. 'Sitting in the chair', 'Eating breakfast', 'Mummy is saying goodbye to Charlie. Goodbye Charlie. Charlie (pointing at Charlie) say goodbye to Mummy (pointing to Mummy). Goodbye Mummy (pointing from Charlie to Mummy).' If the same words and phrases are used repeatedly, learning will happen, perhaps slowly, but learning nevertheless.

Echolalia

Echolalia is the repetition of a word, words, phrase or whole sentences recently heard or even spoken by the child themselves. It is usually most noticeable when immediate but can be delayed. Immediate echolalia seems to be a quick recall of information from short-term memory and superficial processing and may be related to working MEMORY difficulties. At times, children will repeat the phrase and, if a question, subsequently answer it. For example, 'Do you want a story?' repeated by the child as 'Do you want a story?' and almost immediately answered 'Yes, I want a (particular) story.' It appears that the immediate response follows with simple repetition without understanding. As the understanding process occurs in working memory, the response is available to being made appropriate to the earlier comment. In delayed echolalia the child may repeat words, phrases or sentences after a delay that can be anywhere from hours to days later. Immediate echolalia can be indicative of ASD but is not necessarily the case. In ASD, there are self-echoes, other-person echoes or impersonal echoes. Some echolalia may show pronoun or syntax changes. Asked 'What are you doing?' a child may echo 'What am I doing?'

It is perhaps indicative of how people with ASD who may be high functioning seem to develop speech and learn through acquiring phrases rather than single words alone, which may incline them to perseverative SPEECH. The same processes may be implicated in them rigidly installing information that may be inaccurate but to which they then become committed.

Emotions and regulation

As soon as we are born, we start to develop the ability to understand and express emotions. At around two months of age, most babies are able to express themselves with facial expressions and laughter, encouraged by those watching who make likeable or rewarding sounds in return. They are also able to show signs of fear through turning away or crying. These responses are probably learned in the womb when, through 'Operant Conditioning', certain nice sounds may be experienced together (paired) with Mum generating some pleasurable neurotransmitters (perhaps the hormones and neurotransmitters dopamine, oxytocin and vasopressin) that may cross the placental barrier. Similarly, unpleasant sounds may be linked to disturbing neurotransmitters (perhaps cortisol and adrenaline or epinephrine).

By 12 months after birth, most typical infants can read facial expressions (see FACIAL BLINDNESS) and, through social learning, understand what you may be feeling. Most children start to use words to express their feelings when they are toddlers similarly linked by others' approvals and the related neurotransmitters. As typical children continue to grow and develop throughout childhood and adolescence, they learn to empathise, recognise and respond to other people's feelings, are more able to see other people's perspectives (see THEORY OF MIND) and develop self and emotion regulation skills. Children and adults with ASD seem to be 'wired' differently so even as infants they do not learn socially (as in social learning theory) in the same way. There is evidence that they do not have either or both of quite the same genetic inclination (programming) and/ or neurogenesis/development (brain hardware) to attend to human faces and also, as a result, may quite often have difficulty in recognising and distinguishing people from each other.[36] Perhaps because in their early years they don't attend to parents' faces initially and then similarly don't attend to other people to the same extent as typical children, they have difficulty recognising facial expressions probably as a result of not really observing them.

Not recognising other people's emotion-related facial expressions increases the complexity of identifying emotions in themselves and in others. Being unaware of this human trait they then fail to understand the tiny differences in others' words and expressions, important subtleties of communication and social cues. Not recognising their own emotional states, they then have problems with self-regulation. Even much older adults with ASD may still be unable to recognise their emotional states as, for example, shouting in obvious anger, 'I'm not angry!' Due to their struggles with understanding and interpreting emotions, they may come across as lacking in EMPATHY or not having the ability to see the other's point of view.

Being unable to discern emotions in others and perhaps not learning the cues for oneself will make it difficult to regulate or control what is not recognised as an issue.

Frequently, mature adults with ASD can only differentiate between feeling content or upset. They are quite unable to distinguish graduations (see DEPRESSION). Most children never move beyond these two emotions, even with years of professional help. It is known that many children with ASD may be able to learn a long list of words for emotions but may be quite unable to describe the emotions, act them out or recognise them in pictures or in other people acting them out. They can be taught to attend to other people's expressions and tone and as a result come to identify when they are content or upset. As a result they can learn simple strategies to deal with upsets. Most people with ASD are unable to distinguish between ANXIETY and anger or recognise happiness or joy, even when they show it. It is not unusual for a person with ASD being told that they look happy to respond with, 'Why?'

Emotional regulation is a long, complex journey for people with ASD. While they may and do seem to either learn, spontaneously or deliberately, to hide their more extreme signs of emotion, this does not help them to deal with the underlying feelings. They may be severely depressed without any outward signs. In children, this may result in self-harm behaviours (see HARM). Any approach first of all needs to help them understand what emotions are and how they appear in others, then help them simply recognise contentment or upset and appropriate strategies. One means of doing this is SILENT FILMS.

Empathy

People with ASD are said to find it most difficult to understand what others may be thinking or feeling. This is probably an understatement. They may never have even understood that they should attend to facial expressions (see FACIAL BLINDNESS) and contexts, perhaps not having had the genetic 'programming' to do so, although the research on this is far from settled. Unless they were instructed to do so at an early age and assisted in developing strategies as to how to do it, they may be quite unable to decipher other people's expressions. Many people with ASD may become anxious even when just told to make EYE CONTACT, let alone to concertedly look at other people's faces. They may also become so mired in the details and facts of surroundings that they are unable, and again perhaps not 'programmed', to attend to feelings, including their own.

In order to be responsive to someone, we need to be able to interpret the contextual, social, behavioural and emotional cues that indicate their needs and emotional state. In people with ASD this inability is not a lack of empathy but a perceptual disability. When people with ASD have situations explained to them, in terms they can understand, they are most likely to exhibit heartfelt emotional responses. One way to think of this is to imagine looking at sunlight through leaves. The sunlight can overwhelm one's vision so that the leaves are indiscernible. Another is the often mistranslated and mis-stated original famous phrase of Gestalt psychologist Kurt Koffkai:[37] 'The whole is *other* than the sum of the parts.'[38] Many people with ASD may have difficulty in perceiving the whole. There is most interesting quite old research by a namesake, von der Heydt, and colleagues in Zurich into visual illusions or 'illusory contours'. In their paper[39] they use a 'virtual' triangle, indicated only by three black circles with a wedge removed (see image).

Most typical people have no difficulty in perceiving the triangle when asked only, 'What geometric shape do you see?' Children with ASD most often describe it as three Pac-Man shapes[40] or three pieces of pie. An engineer once told me 'I know what you want me to say, but I can never see these things,' and went on to describe all the other optical illusions he could not see. It seems highly likely that the perceptual system of people with ASD works differently.

An additional challenge for people with ASD is their difficulty in appreciating the perspective of another person if different from their own, called THEORY OF MIND. They may not even recognise that another person has the same view they have or have a concept that people have a particular view at all. They may be brusque in rejecting another perspective as not having the ability to conceive of this human attribute; they may just see the other as irrational or stupid and may say this to their face, even if they themselves are wrong. Because people with ASD *appear* to lack empathy through misinterpreting situations, they may seem cold, unkind or selfish. By attending to and recognising facial expressions, face-reading skills and empathy can be taught to help them understand other people's cues and how to act in particular situations. Starting this early when their brains are still developing is most important. (See also SILENT FILMS.)

Encopresis – see Defecating and Toileting

Enuresis – see Urinating and Toileting

Executive function

Executive function is an umbrella term used to describe the management of thought (cognitive) processes including organising, planning, sustaining attention, thinking flexibly, initiating responses, inhibiting inappropriate responses, shifting attention, short-term memory, emotion regulation (see EMOTIONS AND REGULATION) and even MOTOR SKILLS. Many people with ASD experience problems with executive function that can interfere with their daily interactions and activities. They may have trouble with organising themselves and planning, which can negatively impact on their ability to engage in daily living activities. Others may become obsessed to the extent that they need to organise every aspect of their lives and those of their family, to a similarly dysfunctional conclusion. While some may be very good with attention to detail, they may fail to see the bigger picture. It can be akin to trying to walk forward while staring intently at one's toes. Walking into something or tripping becomes a serious risk. They may also struggle to organise their thoughts and actions and have poor impulse control. Executive function may also explain some difficulties with THEORY OF MIND and even regulation of emotions as well as the most complex area of conceptual blindness (see CREATIVITY AND CONCEPTUAL BLINDNESS).

Quite often ATTENTION DEFICIT HYPERACTIVITY DISORDER is seen as emblematic of executive function difficulties, but this may just be another one among many. The most likely indicators from IQ tests are found in the results for FLUID REASONING as well as working MEMORY. A particular difficulty of executive function combined with the emotional centres of the brain may be OCD. Assessments of executive function should be included when assessing for ASD as it indicates where alternative functional strategies may be important in the child's life. They are usually conducted by clinical psychologists to identify areas requiring support and can help in formulating strategies to do so.

Exposure and Response Prevention (ERP)

This is a particular therapeutic approach used by professionals, mostly clinical psychologists, with people with OBSESSIVE COMPULSIVE DISORDER. The approach follows research that shows a helpful change can be achieved as subjects confront their fears in a safe way, even though it may make them feel extremely uncomfortable and cause great anxiety at the time. They are prevented from activating their typical emotional 'escape' response such as hand-washing or checking or counting. The behavioural process is called Pavlovian or Classical extinction. An example of this process: a person repeatedly checks light switches to ensure they're in the off position, even when entering a room that is clearly dark and after previously having checked them several times – repeated checking often follows ritual formulas such as the number three and if they become anxious that they may have miscounted, they may insist on counting to seven. It is easy to imagine how this could progress to taking an entire day. In therapy, the person would be exposed to their fear (leaving lights switched on) and would themselves refuse or be prevented from responding to the safety behaviour of checking the switches. As this type of therapy typically causes some short-term increased anxiety, it is necessary for it to be done by experienced and trained professionals. Over time, ERP facilitates a long-term reduction in obsessive and compulsive symptoms.

Eye contact

No book about ASD would be complete without some information about eye contact. It, or its absence, is often used as one of the key informal criteria, and all too often incorrectly as a formal criterion, for determining whether someone has ASD or to exclude them from a diagnosis. The cause of a lack of eye contact from *some* people with ASD may be that their brains have a deficit in the area of specialisation for facial recognition (see FACIAL BLINDNESS). As a result, from birth, they may lack some or all of the 'programming' or 'wiring' to attend to or recognise human faces as distinct from other objects. They may also not enjoy being looked at for any reason, or become anxious when they are, a trait that many people without ASD share, not liking to be the centre of attention. This may be compounded by cultural habits, such as Australian Aborigines who, unrelated to ASD, consider it rude to stare at or be stared at by others. When conducting a conversation or therapy, with all Indigenous Australians, it is always more appropriate to sit alongside than opposite them. This is often also helpful in children with ASD.

People with ASD may have been told from an early age to 'Look at me!' when talking, and so they develop a number of techniques to disguise their dislike of eye contact. These may, paradoxically, include staring at the other person and sometimes even in a most disconcerting, unblinking way but not focusing. They may use techniques such as staring at noses, chins or hair. They may also use quite surreptitious glances from under their brows or glide their gaze past from one side to the other.

Any effort at early correction of this may result in significant increases in anxiety with resultant possible challenging and unwanted BEHAVIOUR such as MELTDOWNS. Is it necessary or worth it?

F

Facial blindness

People with ASD tend to have difficulty reading and understanding facial expressions. For some people, this may seem very confusing and overwhelming, making it most challenging for them to understand social interactions. As they struggle to interpret various facial expressions they may misunderstand what the other person is communicating, which can result in inappropriate or confusing responses from the person with ASD. When you are interacting with your child, be mindful of how you use your speech and gestures in your communication. You could even help your child by explaining what your facial expressions mean by breaking them down and labelling the appropriate feelings for each. There are strategies which a clinical psychologist can help you use in your home with your child.

Research suggests that people with autism struggle with understanding and interpreting facial expressions because they have problems with processing the visual information associated with facial recognition.[41] The fancy word is prosopagnosia, which seems to be present in most people with ASD to different extents. It does appear that there is a 'wiring' difference at birth, which does not 'programme' people with ASD to observe faces to the same extent as typical children.[42] Clinicians and parents become quite aware of the differences between the way ASD infants may even strain and become upset in an effort to avoid eye contact while typical infants seem to stare unblinkingly and pull cute faces to attract warm responses. Your child may also have trouble recognising and distinguishing faces and may need help in finding other ways to help recognise people such as by clothing, nose, hairstyle or glasses. Some children with ASD may give the appearance of typical eye contact or even staring, but on enquiry they may be looking at noses, chins or, as one child described, 'scrunching, so it's blurred'.

Reciprocally, not having spontaneously learned the meaning of others' expressions or not having an intrinsic understanding of mimicking, mirroring or modelling others, many children with ASD may have quite bland expressions or, the opposite, highly expressive but indecipherable expressions. These include frowning or grimacing, lifting individual eyebrows, seemingly quizzically but not so intended, and all of these are usually quite unconscious.

They may also have even more unusual or inappropriate expressions. Frequently, even though avoiding eye contact, they may stare intensely. An extremely clever young medical specialist with ASD was encouraged to obtain help for the fixed stare she used with patients, which they were finding intimidating. She was quite oblivious.

An adult with ASD was observed to be gently holding his tiny baby daughter but with the most anguished and apparently grief-stricken expression. It invoked a profound distress and sense of dread in the people nearby that something really terrible had happened. When he was approached quietly and sensitively and asked if everything was alright, his expression became even more of a grimace and frankly ugly, as he held his daughter out for examination and asked rhetorically, 'Isn't she just so beautiful?' His expression was of extreme emotion and love but it did not appear so. (See SILENT FILMS for a strategy.)

Faecal smearing and other unwanted behaviour

Faecal smearing is a topic that most people dread, and very few parents of children with autism like to talk about. While this only occurs in a few children with ASD and may also occur in children with other disabilities, there are quite a few with ASD who have a tendency to enjoy smearing their own poop in different places. There is no definitive answer as to why children with ASD engage in faecal smearing; however, it seems likely, and many clinicians believe, that playing with their own faeces may be a sensorily satisfying experience. The children usually exhibit the signs of pleasure when doing so, including giggling and laughter. How you react may also be reinforcing their behaviour, which means that they may be doing this for the response it attracts. It can be most trying for already stretched and stressed parents, as well as unhygienic.

Health professionals understand that this can be an embarrassing and difficult subject to discuss but it is important that you talk about it as there may be, and usually are, some simple strategies with which they can help you to correct this behaviour. These may include demonstrating appropriate ways of dealing with faeces from animals and humans, namely, down the toilet or in a bin. Depending on age, providing children with a distraction that occupies their hands while they are toileting (favoured toy or play dough or a game) engages their hands away from their rears. Rewarding correct flushing of faeces, perhaps with a small ceremony such as 'bye bye poo' can also be successful, as can taking the mystery out of adult toileting providing an opportunity for children to learn socially. (See TOILETING for further information.)

Fight–flight (and freeze) (see also Anxiety)

This is closely related to challenging BEHAVIOUR. Most people have heard of the fight, flight and also the freeze responses. These are the result of the survival-driven fear instinct that has allowed animals (including humans) to endure and thrive at different levels on the food chain. This is a function of the marvellously integrated central nervous system. It is no more, and probably much less, strange for a child to react with 'fight' (hitting) and 'flight' (BOLTING) in relation to a perceived threat, than it is for a very intelligent and high functioning typical university student sitting an examination in a comfortable and safe room to react with an animal-like 'freeze' response to the perception of threat to their future through failing an examination.

There is poorly understood knowledge that children with ASD have *dis*similar cortisol times and rates of production compared with typical children. Most people experience a doubling of their cortisol levels on waking, which allows them to prepare for their day. They also exhibit aroused levels at times of changing activities. It may be a consequence of this different production of cortisol by the adrenal glands that children with ASD are, literally, physically less able to transition at any time of the day.

It has long been understood, but not always effectively implemented, that the proper way to overcome fight and flight is to, *where possible*, and it isn't always, understand and address the direct causes triggering the reacting, so as to prevent them arising. For many of the children who react with fight and/or flight (a natural sympathetic nervous system function), it may have been a distracting whisper in the back of the class, the recall of an inadvertent or deliberate push in the playground that day or last year, or that the teacher asked another student for a response when the child who reacted also knew the answer. Identifying the triggers can be the key to helping repair the *immediate* problem. Effective strategies to do this are 'walk-throughs' (active re-enactments while ensuring not triggering distress) and Carol Gray's 'Comic Strip Conversations'.[43] These, though, are only solutions to specific problems and do not address the complexity of directing your child to learn and exhibit always-appropriate behaviour. For that a comprehensive, coherent and active strategy is essential. One approach is through, for example, EARLY INTERVENTION and APPLIED BEHAVIOUR ANALYSIS.

It is important to understand that aggression by a child or teenager is seldom intended to cause distress in others (except in very rare cases where the distress of others has been paired with a benefit, such as, hitting another child results in a suspension and going home to watch TV or play video games). Its purpose, at least initially, is to reduce their stress and anxiety and meet their needs and increase the likelihood of their survival. To do so, children will start by using the examples of others as they are able to interpret them. After a while, though, the behaviour may become habitual. It may also change if the child doesn't perceive it as obtaining the desired outcome. It may also be influenced by other factors so that its relationship becomes impossible to disentangle. It is really important to understand the many possible triggers for the anxiety or unease and, as parents and carers, anticipate them and develop strategies to cope with or avoid them.

Think of what may cause distress to us as mature adults. There are innumerable such situations inviting the deliberately odd examples that are provided here. They include those occasions where we are unsure of what is happening; or perhaps we may feel it is critical to make our needs understood by others and we are unable to do so, perhaps raising fears for our continued wellbeing. Examples are perhaps looking for a parking space, being caught in a noisy crowd, missing out on a bargain or needing to use a toilet when its availability is not obvious or immediately accessible. These examples may sound silly but they are no more or less a part of the human condition than a mature adult terrified to the point of jumping on a coffee table and screaming at a *photograph* of a three-centimetre long Australian marsupial mouse, which usually attracts comments of 'It's so cute!'

There are also situations of typical anxiety. One of the most common anxiety-provoking behaviours is making a speech, often causing the preparatory flight reaction of trembling. Another is fear of flying. These seem completely different, and yet our response is the same. The first is obviously harmless while the second is only very remotely likely to be dangerous and much less likely to cause death than, for example, choking on food.[44] *Please note:* This example should never be told to a child with ASD, as they may easily become obsessed (see OCD) with choking. A single sneeze can initiate an obsession with germs that may take years to eliminate.

Film (social skills development technique) – see Silent films

Fluid reasoning

A human ability present in most of us is that of being able to reason in different ways. Typically, *deductive reasoning* is referred to as 'bottom up', an example of which is seeing a child with a particular behaviour, such as flapping, and trying to determine what may be their particular difficulty; while *inductive reasoning* is 'top down', perhaps trying to understand the difficulties of children with ASD.

There are other types of reasoning, namely, *abductive* and *heuristic*. Only very briefly, in our example of a child with certain behaviours, abductive reasoning should result in the development of a theory of what is happening to cause the behaviour. That may be a view that the child is sleep deprived, anxious or has a difference in their brain. This is the approach most often used by medical professionals. Heuristic reasoning is best described as an 'educated guess'; having learned something in the past, we may make a guess in a different situation. An example may be baking a cake when we have previously experienced that if we follow a particular recipe, then the cake won't rise. Knowing about baking powder, we guess that adding a little more than is suggested in the recipe will fix the problem.

Fluid reasoning is the term used by psychologists to cover these abilities and they are usually assessed using IQ and other tests (see ASSESSMENTS). Children with ASD often have great difficulty in reasoning, being best at deductive reasoning. Even in deductive reasoning they can make errors of logic or use deductive reasoning when they should be using inductive reasoning. An example of a deductive error was a child who saw the film *Jurassic Park* and therefore wanted to go and see the dinosaurs. When told it was just a film and not real, the child was unable to understand this, insisting for many years that dinosaurs were around, having seen them in a film.

Another difficulty is the problem of decision making, and in particular that of *arbitrary* DECISIONS. The problem is simply how can someone who is strictly logical decide between two things that are identical? The example given is of a person with ASD choosing, through 'logical' reasoning which is their preferred style, which of two identical cans of beans to buy. The only way around this for people with this disability, common in ASD and some types of brain injury, is to have an arbitrary rule. The circularity of this reasoning is obvious. How can one possibly arrive at an arbitrary rule about arbitrary decisions? I hope you aren't getting a headache. The answer is that someone else needs to simply, concisely, decisively and authoritatively provide the rule. One approach to the described conundrum is to always select the item at the front, on the top at left. Once, a person with ASD encountered a problem with this approach in buying an apple from a large box of apples. Each time they selected one by applying the rule, another apple would roll into the position. The rule was expanded: continue applying the rule until you have enough of the desired items. These sorts of rules work in most cases and can alleviate high levels of anxiety about everyday tasks.

Food

Food can be a huge issue for children with ASD. They may eat too much or too little. Their body or stomach may not send them typical signals, and so they may even forget to drink fluids on a hot day or to eat when they have not done so for a long time. Some children may need medication for other reasons which may suppress or increase appetite and cause them to lose or gain weight (psycho-stimulants or mood stabilisers, respectively). Then there are all the SENSORY SENSITIVITIES issues they may have around food which are likely to be a source of anxiety.

Generally, mixing foods of different colours, textures, tastes and types on a plate can be a problem. If allowed by the child, often they may not touch each other so that compartmentalised plates such as used by airlines and hospitals can be most helpful.

Foods with inconsistent textures, such as muesli, will be out. Children may like yoghurt and enjoy fruit, but yoghurt with fruit will be rejected. Similar-looking food of different types can add variety. Small mincemeat balls, chicken nuggets, mashed potato balls and round scoops of pumpkin, beetroot and gnocchi may all be regarded as similarly acceptable.

A clever paediatrician, nutritionist or clinical psychologist will be able to assist with improving eating.

Friends and friendship

Making friends is an important part of children's development. For children with ASD, this can be more challenging as they may have trouble with understanding friendship, either not engaging at all or being too dominant in their play. They may struggle with initiating and maintaining a conversation; have difficulty apprehending what others may be thinking or feeling; not know how to join in other children's activities by either not getting the rules or insisting on their own; not be aware to or misread facial expressions and body language; be unable to adjust to unfamiliar and novel social situations or solving social problems such as whose turn, what to do, arguments or bullying.

Can you imagine walking through a car-wash? A child described the first birthday party his parents arranged for him, aged six, with ten guests, as like walking through a car-wash. When the first child arrived, it was just a squirt of water in his eyes. When the second child arrived it, was like soap in his eyes. By the time more children arrived, he felt the brushes and blowers and ran to his room where he hid for the rest of the day. It took professional help and four practices over the next year for him to have a party with five guests. Even then he wanted to know why he couldn't just see them one at a time. He has, for him most happily, not had a party since. He has become adept at attending others' parties, as long as he can leave after, he is now up to, two hours.

You can help your child develop social skills and a degree of social ease by providing them with opportunities to meet other children *one at a time and progressing one by one* and to develop their social skills in controlled ways in natural environments. Positive friendships can help boost your child's self-esteem and confidence, which is important in creating opportunities for them to build their social skills (but please don't expect them to do so spontaneously, as they will not) as well as resilience.

School is often a good place for children to start making friends, *one at a time adding them one by one.* As your child increasingly interacts with other children, be sure to keep your eye out for signs of BULLYING. Informal but highly organised play dates, organised social groups in everyday environments such as parks, school playgrounds and homes are more natural and more directly transportable than therapy groups in artificial surroundings.

The Scouting organisation, due to its highly structured nature, can be most attractive even for low ability children with ASD, *with proper support.* Of course, the child and any organisation will need advance advice and support as to what to do and how to behave, and calming strategies including time out – to relax, not as punishment.

For children with ASD, friends can be a confusing concept (see CREATIVITY AND CONCEPTUAL BLINDNESS), and their notions of friends and friendship can confuse their parents and be confused by their parents. Being told at the school gate to have a good time and play with their friends, given conceptual and facial recognition challenges (see FACIAL BLINDNESS), can set them up for years of muddle. When asked how many friends they have, many children with ASD will pick any large number approximating their notion of numbers of children at their school (often, a million). When asked if they have friends in their class they will similarly estimate the number of classmates (hundreds). Again, if asked about close friends, their literal inclination will cause them to describe those who sit close at different times. If more specifically they were to be asked how many they see outside of school time, in their own or the other child's home, they may exhibit increased confusion and ask, 'Why?' Our failure to explain the notion of friendship and our increasing tendency towards social media and in the West towards isolated living, paradoxically within ever-growing cities, makes the concept of friendship increasingly impenetrable. This extends to relationships later in life.

G

Gait (see also Motor skills)

Problems with motor coordination and sensory sensitivities are commonly found in people with ASD. Therefore, it is not surprising that some children may walk with an unusual gait or show numerous gait stereotypes such as pacing, toe-walking, jumping, hopping, skipping and spinning. These stereotypical behaviours have also been referred to as repetitive behaviours. Just to make things less complicated, we will focus on walking patterns. In addition to poor motor control and coordination, low muscle tone or hyper-flexibility can affect how your child walks. You may notice that from a young age they walk differently compared with typical children, are maybe more clumsy and show fewer physical capabilities. If you are concerned about your child's gait, consult with your paediatrician or physiotherapist on how they can improve their gait or address any physical problems associated with this. Radical treatments such as braces and surgery should be considered with great caution and additional professional opinions obtained.

There is an interesting and little-understood side issue. Particular gait and hyper-flexibility can be indicative of differences in learning. As a result, it is suggested that in addition to a paediatrician and physiotherapist, unusual gait should be discussed with an ASD-familiar learning professional or clinical psychologist.

Gender

As your child grows and develops their identity, they may have an inclination to engage in certain activities or behave in ways that in our culture are regarded as 'masculine' or 'feminine'. This may occur in all children from as early as three years. It may be associated with fitting in with their siblings, friends or peers, identifying with a character from a film or book or showing a liking for clothes with certain textures or sensations that are usually worn by the opposite gender (for example, a young boy liking the pretty look or feel of lacy dresses). It may also appear innate in that from the earliest memories of the significant adults in their lives, they describe a predisposition for the child to behave as the other gender. This may have occurred in play, dress, manner and showing affection. As they grow older and begin to learn about what gender means and how this is portrayed in our society and culture, some children become assured of their preference to be another gender. The foregoing applies to all children.

Please note that the comments that follow only apply to children with ASD. People with ASD are only likely to be a small proportion of the transgender community. Some children, and perhaps more so those with ASD, may become confused and unsure about their gender, which can result in experiences of gender dysphoria. Gender dysphoria literally means unhappiness with one's gender. This is not accurate for all. Many children may just have a strong preference for, a desire to be, or wish to emulate another gender to the point of transitioning. It may, in children with ASD, be related to problems of flexible thinking. Having a desire to wear particular clothes, for example, they feel the need to behave as that gender. It also appears to have much to do with identity formation and the difficulties for those with ASD in progressing this through puberty (see CREATIVITY AND CONCEPTUAL BLINDNESS). They may feel more comfortable relating to others who are of the opposite gender and, therefore, they perceive that it is more acceptable to identify themselves with them.

There appear to be two key stages in the developmental continuum when the inclination to a particular gender orientation may change. The first may be as early as at two years and the second at puberty through to late teens. However, it may only be much later that others become aware of the person's gender identity. The confidence, perception of safety and opportunities to 'come out' may be restricted by the person, their social and cultural environment and many other circumstances. It is not unusual for transgender people to only feel comfortable in transitioning much later in their lives. The 'early' transitioners may readily progress and develop to lead satisfactory and fulfilling lives. With support of others and unselfconscious of their transitioning, they may be unaware of societal views until those are irrelevant to their personal journey. They may still, unfortunately, experience difficulties in being accepted by others. For those who recognise their gender orientation later and think to transition, life can be far more challenging and even distressing as they are likely to be so much more aware of societal views and pressures. This may delay their transitioning, causing them enduring and perhaps lifelong distress and regret. It may also be more difficult having begun later and requiring more people to be accommodating, as well as perhaps more complex medical interventions.

Whatever the reasons and whether it leads to gender transitioning, lesbian, gay, neutral, non-binary or any other manifestation of gender, support is essential for children and teens (and all other people) navigating these difficult development processes. As parents, it is important to seek to understand how your child sees themselves and to provide positive support as they develop their sense of IDENTITY, of which gender may be dominant but is only a part. Any lack of appropriate support and absence of accurate information can lead to severe depression, self-harm and, tragically, even suicide.

For understanding, it may be worth appreciating that any person may have several gender identities and inclinations simultaneously, such as birth, identity and sexual genders. They may also have non-stereotypical preferences for their preferred partner's birth, identity and sexual genders. Identity includes our naturally determined or natal gender at birth; our developing personal gender identity; and a developing sexual gender which may be masculine, feminine, both or neither. If these are different to how we are perceived, it can cause distress. In some people, these may be highly specific and limiting, while others may be pan-sexual. If this is confusing for a typical reader, imagine how confusing it may be for someone with

ASD, who may be confused themselves because of the many contradictory signals they receive from their brains, their bodies and the social environment, or are confused only that others are. You may need to re-read this a few times!

For advice, a clinical psychologist or specialist sexual therapist may be helpful.

Gestures (repetitive) (see also Stereotypies)

Some people with ASD engage in repetitive behaviour that may appear strange or unusual to others. The types of repetitive behaviours vary for each individual. Some may only exhibit such behaviours when they are feeling intense emotions such as upset, distressed, angry or excited.

Some may use them to calm themselves. Some exhibit these behaviours in a ritualised manner that can limit their ability to participate in activities that are not part of their routine. Repetitive behaviours seem to begin at age two to three years, but flapping and rocking, for example, may be seen much earlier. During preschool years the behaviour can be extreme and constant; however, as they grow older, the ritual behaviours may become less apparent. Therapy can be helpful in reducing or eliminating repetitive behaviours which are inappropriate or harmful, such as head banging.

It is essential to ask yourself how important it is to eliminate the behaviour, as it may be a source of comfort or calming, and its elimination my result in a different and potentially worse behaviour. This is directly demonstrated in the excellent documentaries *Autism: Extreme Love*, presented by Louis Theroux.[45] Often, allowing the child to continue their non-harmful behaviour may be the best approach. On the other hand, children may use this to avoid attending to or attempting participation in benign aspects of their everyday world. To help them learn new skills, the temporary stopping of the behaviour may be necessary. A reinforcer of TOKEN REWARD SYSTEMS may be allowing them to use their self-stimulatory behaviour for a fixed time.

A harmful behaviour can usually be adapted to something similar but harmless. Modifying the behaviour may allow children to be less restricted in their activities and participate more freely. Some common repetitive behaviours seen in people with autism include: hand or arm flapping, twirling, rocking, clenching muscles, repeating a noise or phrase in a certain way, flicking fingers, head banging and finger tapping.

Girls

As difficult as it is for boys, ASD can be more problematic for girls and women. This is, in perhaps a large part, reinforced by mental health and medical professionals perhaps not knowing as much about autism as they should. While it used to be said, and even recently, that only one in four people with ASD was female, the gap of diagnosing ASD in women is narrowing. Many young to older women may have attracted diagnoses of bipolar disorder (BD) and borderline personality disorder (BPD) which, when seen in males, would have been diagnosed as ASD. This occurs to the present, unfortunately. Women who have appeared unusual by the stereotypical standards of society may also have been inappropriately misdiagnosed, often through their lack of interest in typical female pursuits or on the basis of self-harm (see HARM) or a suicide attempt. On self-harm, perhaps other forms of emotional expression should not be surprising in people unable to recognise or communicate their emotional state. Typically, they do not experience the self-harm as painful. There are many clinical examples including mathematicians, a rock musician, a motor mechanic, electricians, plumbers, engineers, a cyber-security expert and scientists who have originally been diagnosed with BD and BPD. Subsequent, much later, reviews have identified ASD but often only after many years of inappropriate treatment, which may have caused suffering through enforced hospitalisation, medication and even electro-convulsive therapy. Quite often for such women, being given a new understanding of their difficulties has in itself resulted in significant functional improvement.[46]

The continuing disservice to girls with ASD is framed through the adherence to the limited nature of the formal diagnosis of ASD, with no condition supposed to include every manifestation of a disorder and exclude every other. Someone with depression may also have had an amputation, but this does not form part of the diagnosis, in particular subsequently to the DSM-IV-TR.[47]

By focusing on social skills, where women may be more adept (and this is debatable), the presence of ASD may be missed. It seems that increasing testosterone in boys and related challenging behaviour may facilitate a diagnosis at the onset of puberty. Girls at this age display very different behaviours, due in a large part to oestrogen and progesterone.

Clinical experience suggests that by adulthood most women with ASD have received some diagnosis; just not necessarily the correct or most helpful diagnosis. The diagnosis of BPD seems to be often applied because many women (as do men) with ASD may actually, in spite of the popular mythology, not have great social skills and may even be socially inept or use inappropriate strategies to make friends by trying to end other friendships (as do men). They may be depressed and talk about suicide (as do men) and may self-harm (as do men).

It seems that due to men in the past having mostly used more dangerous methods of attempting suicide than women, and sadly been more successful, and used more violent and therefore more obvious methods of self-harm, they have attracted different diagnoses. It has been quite obvious over many years that where women and men may have almost identical difficulties, symptoms and functioning, they will usually attract different diagnoses. As guidelines suggest that BPD may not be diagnosed until early adulthood, a canvassing of the early experiences of a child should properly indicate the presence of ASD. This may need school visits by the clinician, not necessarily taking the child's view that they have 'hundreds of friends' (see FRIENDS AND FRIENDSHIP).

H

Harm (self and other)

Self-harming is most distressing to the family of the child or teen who is harming but paradoxically is more often seen by them as alleviating anxiety. The prevalence of this, mostly in adolescents but also children, is thought to be around 15 per cent.[48] Its prevalence in children with ASD is unknown. It can take many forms such as deliberate cutting and burning, of limbs mostly, head banging against really hard surfaces or with fists, biting, hair pulling, nail biting, penetrating skin with sharp objects, ingesting objects (pica[49]) or consuming pills or poison, self-asphyxiation and others. Anecdotally it has increased in frequency through social media, where the subject is openly discussed by teenagers on thousands of sites. Children as young as five have been known to access such sites out of curiosity though, fortunately, as far as we know, not copied the behaviour. It is nevertheless only a matter of time, and as for any number of reasons, children's internet use should always be supervised.

Why mostly teens self-harm is a much researched but little clarified topic. Even many discussions with young people who are actively self-harming may only result in 'I feel better' or 'It feels good', but for the most part 'I don't know' responses.

The best explanation seems to be that it allows an expression of emotions that cannot be communicated, a major issue in ASD, as well as perhaps a mood-justifying physical sensation from the harming.

Strategies to reduce self-harm include distraction, other behaviours such as flicking a rubber band around a wrist, a contract to reduce the incidence to once a week and only with someone in attendance. The best news is that most young people survive their self-harm and grow out of it. Medication may assist but which and in what situations is far from obvious. Obtaining ANIMALS to care for has shown some benefit although those preferred may not always be animals that families will accept, often for some reason being snakes and rats.

Effective therapy is that of EXPOSURE AND RESPONSE PREVENTION. Another approach used in the early stages of treatment may be Motivational Interviewing, a therapeutic approach to encourage and strengthen motivation to change troubling behaviour.[50]

Unfortunately children and teens (and adults with ASD) *will also hurt others*. Many families seem to attempt to accommodate this in early years when it is most easily improved and only decide later to seek professional and official help (see PROFESSIONALS). It is immensely distressing for a family to have to call the police or ambulance to attend to a loved family member, and perhaps even more so knowing they have ASD. Individual police dislike attending such call-outs and all too often their presence can escalate the situation. Police have very strict regulations to follow and rightly will not put themselves into harm's way if they can avoid it. If parents have a potentially violent child, they should develop a relationship with local police, including offering to have their psychologist provide a brief presentation. It is also helpful if the police can meet the child at a time when there are no issues, so that the child can preferably become understanding of their presence while CALM. Usually a child with ASD will be unable to differentiate one officer from another (see FACIAL BLINDNESS). If this is the case then the police attendance is much more likely to be successful in reducing rather than increasing the child's distress. Once called, their advice should be followed.

A child's possible tendency to lash out needs professional help from the very first occasion. *Delaying seeking help, for whatever reason, the most common being embarrassment, will likely result in a deterioration of the situation.*

Hearing (see also Language and Speech)

Extremely sensitive hearing is one of the abilities of many children with ASD, and this can be quantified with testing. They also seem possibly more prone to ear infections than typical peers, although for no discernible reason. It may be that they don't draw attention to early indications of ill health. Even though they may have excellent hearing, this is only one aspect of LEARNING and being properly able to interpret what they hear can be problematic. Hearing is not the same as understanding, and deriving information from heard speech can be difficult and meaning and nuance may be lost. Many children with ASD, during language development, seem to be unable to differentiate words in sentences. ECHOLALIA is a common trait of children and adults with ASD and may be indicative of how they hear and acquire LANGUAGE.

As they grow, they may suffer what is often called 'cocktail party syndrome', where they are unable to differentiate speech of an individual if there is anyone else talking or there are other distractions.

Humour

People with ASD may not understand or appreciate sarcasm or subtlety and may not understand jokes the way others do. When they try to be funny, it can come off as awkward, gauche, socially inappropriate or even aggressive. They need to have this pointed out to them gently. Usually, the humour enjoyed by people with ASD can be quite crass or 'slapstick'.

There can be complex issues about what children with ASD perceive to be humorous and what is their motivation. In the middle of his first year of school, Laz accidentally tripped and fell against his teacher from behind, who steadied him. His classmates laughed. Laz had made no friends during the year and had some rejection following inappropriately interfering in their class activities and play. Following his fall against the teacher, over the next days and weeks he repeatedly pretended to trip or fall, but his peers quickly lost interest. He again, this time deliberately, fell against his teacher, who recognised his motivation and admonished him. Nevertheless, his classmates again laughed. Laz understood that it was his contact with the teacher that made them laugh. He progressively commenced assaulting his teacher, first by bumping into her and eventually by touching her bottom, for which he was sent to the Principal. Egged on by his classmates, he then tried to touch his teacher's breast. Obviously this highly inappropriate behaviour needed to be addressed. This showed no results, until they attended a psychologist who engaged with the whole class, making Laz's good behaviour all of their responsibility, with positive reinforcement when he did behave well. With some explanation, even these five- and six-year-old children changed their accommodation of and support for Laz.

In adults with ASD, similar experience has them being the joker at work or social events, confusingly for them provoking both positive and negative responses. On occasion this has resulted in them being fired from their jobs.

I

Identity (and how it is developed)

It is extremely optimistic to try to explain identity in such a brief summary. If the topic interests you, you are encouraged to read some of the references appended. These are, for the most part, intended to be quite easily understood.

Philosophers have put forward their ideas in relation to identity for centuries. For most children, developing an identity is something that spontaneously begins at birth and progressively develops as a uniqueness, of which they are largely unaware. There is a well-established theory as to the confusion that children and adults experience between their role and identity. This is often seen most prominently through adolescence and during the so-called mid-life crisis. The role is how people act and what they do, where identity is the person or core that remains constant between the roles – sometimes seen as being behind a mask. If this is difficult to grasp, imagine how impossible it may be for someone who can't even begin to imagine what identity is, in part due to their young age but also the conceptual blindness prevalent in ASD (see CREATIVITY AND CONCEPTUAL BLINDNESS).

The difficulty for children with ASD is that they approach the world in a concrete or literal way. Various family members will each have a different view of the child and whether perhaps they are smart, courteous, disciplined, hard-working and cooperative or dumb, rude, naughty, lazy and disobedient. Imagine the confusion for a child where one parent may call them smart and another dumb, or a teacher telling them they are rude and a grandparent that they are polite. While all people face these difficulties, children with ASD don't have any sense of who they are beyond the way they are described by others. One of the common 'insults' currently in the playground is calling someone 'gay'. Imagine how confusing this may be to a child who is also told by a family member that they are just like their father or mother.

Identity confusion can be one of the most distressing and damaging issues for children with ASD and a serious impediment to self-confidence, self-esteem and what Albert Bandura called self-efficacy or the ability to act and be effective and comfortable in society.[51] These are potentially the foundations of depression and anxiety. It is extremely difficult to help even high functioning and intelligent adults with ASD to appreciate their own centrality to their lives and not just as a ball in everyone else's soccer game. Some adults become inclined to see themselves as preferentially in a single role. The workaholic ignores her family and cannot understand why they resent her. The football-addicted father cannot understand why work colleagues and the family don't endorse and support his interests exclusively. A father made his ballet-loving child play his favourite sport, rugby.

Identity needs to be progressively and continually explained and demonstrated to children with ASD in simple and constructive ways. The SILENT FILMS approach can help by inviting them to describe what they like or dislike about certain characters. 'What did you like about Elsa/Nemo?', or 'What behaviour did you like about Elsa/Nemo?', or 'What values did you see in Elsa/Nemo?', depending on age and the films and video being watched. This may need to be massaged to meet your expectations. Also use the opposites or dark characters, 'What didn't you like about Cruella/Thunderclap?', or 'What behaviour didn't you like about Cruella/Thunderclap?', or 'What bad values did you see in Cruella/Thunderclap?'

A *values chest* (a decorated box or drawer) can be helpful in this regard. Perhaps divided into two, pictures and photos from any source, souvenirs, everyday items and words on cards, if appropriate to the child, can be placed in it and reviewed with the child, perhaps on addition of each positive (will be) or negative (won't be) value. Given the difficulty with PERFECTIONISM in children with ASD and their great difficulty with nuance or subtlety, it is unhelpful to emphasise what may be impossible, for example, 'Always be good'. The ability to understand this is most dependent on developmental age. The statement is most unhelpful because it requires specificity. A much better value may be 'I will follow good behaviour rules' or 'I will follow rules to be polite' and develop a progressive list of desirable behaviours. This still needs to be mitigated by blind adherence being impossible. 'We can only do our best' and 'There is no such thing as perfect, only doing our best' may also need their place in the values chest.

For children with ASD it is immeasurably important to avoid anything but simple positive direction, and practical and constructive criticism. Compliment them often when due; provide them with the opportunity and encouragement to try new experiences progressively and with increasing difficulty; and help them avoid serious failure, which being literal they are likely to see as personal and irremediable. Challenging behaviour arises where this isn't being stringently pursued even with children more profoundly affected by ASD.

Following the rules Stay Positive, Keep It Simple, Keep It Calm and No Failures is most likely to lead to a contented and appropriately confident child and a relaxed and enjoyable family, social and school environment.

This is often demonstrated when parents live apart. The child's behaviour can be greatly different in one household compared with the other, with all other factors being equal.

Idiosyncrasies (see also Quirky)

People with ASD often see the world in ways that are very different to how most people see things. Professor Temple Grandin, a renowned animal behaviourist with ASD, refers to herself as an 'Anthropologist on Mars'.[52] As many people with ASD have great attention to detail, they may notice many things which others may miss. Neuroscience research shows that the pattern of connectivity in ASD brains can be very different to typical brains.[53] Scientists believe that this is why people with ASD engage in behaviours that are repetitive or seem odd to other people. All of these idiosyncrasies can contribute to people with ASD being seen as quirky, eccentric and having unusual personality traits. While ASD may make them unique and may have helped in their developing some incredible abilities, disabilities in their communication, social and emotional functioning and other common areas of ability such as flexibility and other types of MEMORY may cause them significant difficulties throughout their lives. The early understanding of the unique ways in which their brain works and implementation of appropriate strategies to compensate for or work around weaknesses is their best chance for a contented and satisfying life. (See also ASSESSMENTS.)

Impulsivity

Children with ASD, while known to have limited mental flexibility and preferring routine, can also be worryingly impulsive. They may suddenly wander off or bolt somewhere, hit out while seemingly unprovoked, or without warning have a meltdown. The likelihood is that the matter of concern has been in their thoughts for a while and in some cases this may be for ages. One family visited grandparents each year at Christmas. The grandfather smoked cigarettes. On a repeat visit when other family members were just greeting each other, Clint, who has ASD and SELECTIVE MUTISM, walked straight up to his grandfather and punched him before running off. Two weeks later, using a technique called 'Comic Strip Conversations' (invented by Carol Gray), Clint's psychologist was able to work out that this happened because Clint remembered from his previous visit that his grandfather 'stinks'.

Inappropriateness

People with ASD struggle with social understanding (see SOCIAL SKILLS), so they may say or do things which may be perceived by other people as inappropriate or awkward. They may have trouble fitting in or relating to other people in their life as they may struggle with interpreting social cues or knowing how to respond. Some have trouble with impulse control (see IMPULSIVITY) and flexibility in their thinking, which can make it hard for them stop themselves from saying or doing things that are considered socially inappropriate. (See also HUMOUR.)

Inflexibility

One of the many issues with which people with ASD struggle is flexibility. You may notice that your child has restricted interests and routines as well as obsessions. This is intrinsic to the diagnosis. It is rooted in EXECUTIVE FUNCTION difficulties. They may insist on the factually founded nature and permanence of anything, including SENSORY SENSITIVITIES, the man in the moon or that someone likes or dislikes them. Simply asking your child to shift focus to something else can be very challenging. Trying to help your child see things from a different perspective can be almost impossible (see THEORY OF MIND). The best way in which to do this is through concrete and, again, simple and positive language. Be confident when giving instructions. 'Brush your teeth and go to bed in 15 minutes,' with a reminder at ten and five minutes, rather than, 'Would you like to get ready for bed?' Warnings for shifts in activities are not just preferred by children with ASD but necessary for them to make the required change. Routines work for all children and are essential for children on the spectrum. The chances are that families who try to ignore these needs of children with ASD will have increasing difficulty. There are many other aspects of inflexibility included in this book and with which an ASD professional can help.

Insight

As most typical people develop, they acquire self-awareness or personal insight. For reasons we think are related to the frontal lobe of the brain and conceptual blindness (see CREATIVITY AND CONCEPTUAL BLINDNESS) and perhaps also THEORY OF MIND and FACIAL BLINDNESS, children with ASD, and adults to a greater extent than typical adults, lack personal insight as well as insight into other people and their behaviours. This is the ability to reflect internally, self-monitor and understand themselves and their thoughts, feelings and behaviour as well as consciously think about external people, influences and events. It is very difficult and may be impossible for people with ASD to do this intuitively or spontaneously. However, they can be taught about other people being able to do so. As a result, they can come to accept that it exists in others if told directly and, learning this, they can be assisted to do it deliberately themselves.

This may be most important in relationships between adults where one has ASD. Being able to concretely think about their own and others' thoughts, feelings and behaviour helps them try to understand others and their thoughts, emotions and reasoning. As most people with

ASD get older, they seem to spontaneously develop some knowledge of this without deep understanding. However, they may need assistance throughout their lives in dealing with insight, to them an unfathomable and confusing (and perhaps even unnecessary) aspect of human nature.

Intelligence and IQ

The differences between intelligence and IQ are most confusing. When we talk about intelligence we typically mean how well children and adults can do different things. A child who speaks well or is a good performer at music or at sports may be called intelligent. A good soccer player may be referred to as having good 'field intelligence'. Heston Blumenthal has been called an 'intelligent chef', perhaps with special food or cooking intelligence.

However, when psychologists refer to intelligence they typically mean the intelligence quotient or IQ. This is a measure of a limited number of personal abilities or domains that researchers have found to be generally important for people to be successful in most aspects of life. People often confuse autism with intellectual disabilities. People with ASD have varying levels of intelligence as measured by psychologists. Research in the US in 2014, for example, found that almost half of the children with ASD had average or above-average intelligence. Some people with ASD can have incredible memories, knowledge, thinking and learning skills beyond their age peers but struggle with social and emotional skills. Depending on their neurological make-up, some may have problems with making sense of the information they see (visual processing) or hear (auditory processing), which can make it difficult for them to learn how to read and write. To make things even more complicated, sensory and motor coordination problems can also contribute to their difficulties with LEARNING. Many people with ASD have varying degrees of difficulty in WRITING words by hand while they may be adequate typists.

Some children with ASD can unfortunately have profound intellectual impairment, while a few may have areas of brilliance giving rise to the notion of savant. While some people with ASD do have incredible abilities in uncommon areas, this is unusual, and they most generally have quite common strengths although at times with weakness in other areas of thinking. The most common area of difficulty is FLUID REASONING, and perhaps the second most is working MEMORY which is indicative of executive dysfunction (see EXECUTIVE FUNCTION).

J

Jumping, hopping or toe-walking (see also Gait)

These behaviours are not uncommon among children with ASD. You may have noticed that your child began standing without having ever crawled or only ever belly crawled. Sometimes, children progress to only walking on their toes while others never walk and only jump. Many physical explanations are provided which may be as helpful as trying to strengthen wrists to improve handwriting – that is, not at all. In reported experience, over many years, this seems to often self-correct, perhaps when body size increases to a certain point, but may be entirely due to the further development of the child's brain. Some may never correct, even into adulthood. Jamie Dornan, a Northern Irish actor, explained recently on TV that he only learned that walking on his toes was wrong when learning to dance for a film role at the age of 31. Not only people with ASD toe-walk.[54]

Some children may have trouble walking with a normal gait but may be good runners. This might be a learned habit or relate to problems with motor coordination or sensory issues. It has been said that children like to do this to avoid over-stimulation as a result of walking on their entire foot. As a result they are put through all sorts of well-intended torture to correct. Some of this may be more harmful than good, such as certain types of spinal manipulation. Some children may find that jumping and walking on their toes feels more comfortable to them. Whatever the reason, this is something that should be watched and if it seems to be causing harm can be treated by a health professional such as a paediatric orthopaedic surgeon and/or physiotherapist.

L

Labels – diagnostic (see also Assessments)

Having a child diagnosed with Autism Spectrum Disorder is usually distressing and can be confusing for many parents. To make things even more complicated, as recorded in COMORBIDITY, your child may be experiencing other conditions, adding to the different labels you may hear other people use to describe your child. Some parents may feel that having a child being labelled as 'autistic' or 'Aspie' or 'on the spectrum' is stigmatising, hurtful and upsetting. Others may see these labels as a way of describing the unique set of attributes their child demonstrates. The terms used in this book have been chosen for their greatest acceptance by people with ASD. Even so, it is inevitable that some will not like them. For many parents, knowing that their child's difficulties are related to a diagnosis of ASD can lead to a sense of relief as it helps to better understand their struggles and what they can do to help. While no diagnosis seeks to, or can ever, describe all the attributes of anyone, let alone a child on the autism spectrum with its many variations and complexities, a diagnosis is like an abbreviation or shorthand allowing professionals to understand what it is that they are seeking to improve. For parents, developing their own knowledge of these terms can be helpful. All professionals are prepared to assist in your understanding.

Language (see also Speech and Hearing)

Problems with communication are synonymous with autism.[55] Depending on the severity of the child's symptoms, the level of spoken and gestural effectiveness can vary significantly. Some children may be quite unable to communicate by any means, others may only be able to communicate using non-verbal language, perhaps such as signing or pictorial language aids. Almost any child may be able to progress to develop some language and speech and, at the very least, some form of communicating. It seems quite unpredictable and so all children with ASD should be encouraged and assisted with strategies throughout their lives. Some children have been known to not speak a word until the age of 14 (as described in SELECTIVE MUTISM) or even older and then do so fluently, albeit in a monotone or with an unusual intonation or accent. This is not to suggest for a moment that every child with ASD has the capacity for ordinary speech. This is simply not the case. Even people with autism and intellectual impairment as well as other disabilities may be able to develop spoken language of a sort that can be understood by those close to them and understand what is being said in turn. Those with high functioning ASD may have highly developed speech and language skills. They may, however, use language unusually such as quoting lines from a film or talk with a foreign accent. Often what is called prosody or the tone and rhythm of spoken language are unusual. As discussed under FACIAL BLINDNESS and THEORY OF MIND, children with ASD are usually quite oblivious to social learning, that is, picking up cues from others unless specifically so directed. In some cases they may choose not to speak, also known as SELECTIVE MUTISM. Most language difficulties can be improved to some extent, either with alternative techniques or direct strategies. There are also specific difficulties with speech and understanding others' communications.

Learning

It should not be a surprise that children with ASD learn differently given that we know their brains are wired differently. It is really important for them to be properly cognitively assessed (see ASSESSMENTS), including this aspect. The examples that follow are all this space allows to indicate the importance of developing a proper programme for your child to maximise their abilities and opportunities. While these examples apply to most children with ASD, they also apply to typical children of varying ability.

Other sections of this book that are relevant are FLUID REASONING, WRITING, READING and UNDERSTANDING.

Children with ASD will usually be unable to follow two sets of information simultaneously. If a teacher is displaying an image while talking about it, this will be highly distracting. For the child with ASD they will be unable to absorb the verbal information in real time. They may be examining the detail of the image but are likely unable to absorb either. Paradoxically, a child with ASD may unknowingly remember the information verbatim and be able to quote it much later, albeit with varying understanding.

The better approach is to show the image without comment for a period, then if possible remove it and talk about it. If teaching directly to the image, there will need to be reasonable direction and pauses. 'We are next going to talk about the part of the nervous system called the brain. Look at the diagram and how it sits on top of the spine.' Indicate the area visually. Pause. Continue with the teaching. Pause.

Children on the spectrum usually learn best by rote. While this is obviously applicable to alphabets and multiplication tables, children with ASD need structure for everything, from how to solve quadratic equations to understanding classic poetry and literature. They need similar structure for essays and assignments. To begin with, just breaking down the topic into understandable phrases is a skill that they will have to be taught. If they have not been formally taught grammar, this may be a prerequisite if they are to be successful. Every element of essays should be demonstrated and practised repeatedly.

Questioning is another area of difficulty. Not understanding the question, being unable to discern the answer wanted or just an inability to respond may precipitate anxiety to the point of adversely sensitising even a gifted child with ASD to the whole school environment, resulting in school REFUSAL. The approach of demonstrating should be followed by an instruction 'Now you do it', all the while remembering the key rules: Keep It Calm, Keep It Simple, No Surprises and No Failures.

Lying

Children with ASD are typically and sometimes embarrassingly truthful. It is their nature to tell things how they see them. They can, however, tell lies and can become quite invested in them. The formal term is pseudologia fantastica or 'unreal fantastic logic', described by one researcher and paraphrased here as 'Lying entirely out of proportion to any discernible benefit. It may be extensive and very complicated and may be observed over a period of years or even a lifetime.'[56] Its prevalence outside of people with ASD is unknown, and the author has only seen it in children and adults with ASD, so it may be an indication of being on the spectrum.

One of the ways that it has been seen to arise is that when children with ASD are asked, for example, how they feel, they may respond by saying, 'I don't know.' The response from an unknowing adult may be, 'You must know.' If an authority figure to a literal child with ASD indicates something as a fact, then they take it on board and have to make up the response. This may occur in many ways on many days and therefore becomes a pattern. The child then seeks to anticipate the question by saying something obviously untrue. This in turn attracts a negative response but at least not the impossible question that they could not answer. As a result their strategy is reinforced and on they go.

M

Medication

There are no medications for ASD. At this time there is no cure, unfortunately. Some medications may be used for comorbid conditions such as inattention, sleep difficulties, anxiety, depression, agitation, tics and challenging behaviour (see COMORBIDITY) and are usually used as a last resort but can be essential as in epilepsy. Those most often seen used in children with ASD are anti-depressants, sometimes also used for anxiety, psycho-stimulants, which may be used for inattention and challenging behaviour, mood stabilisers and anti-psychotics which may be used to assist concentration, sleep, anxiety, agitation and challenging behaviour.[57] In practice, while some medication may help parents and teachers, it is highly questionable as to whether there are any beneficial effects for the child.

As all medications have side effects, these need to be fully understood as the treatment may have detrimental outcomes. Anti-depressants usually used for anxiety in ASD can have the opposite effect. Psycho-stimulants can cause significant loss of appetite and weight loss which may not recover after removal of the medication. Mood stabilisers and anti-psychotics can cause significant weight gain, which may remain for life after removal of the medication.

All carers are encouraged to obtain clarification and second opinions, even though they may have confidence in their practitioner. A good practitioner will happily refer to another for a second opinion. Obtaining any opinion from the internet is discouraged. Many people who tell their stories on the internet, with the best intentions, usually are only familiar with their own experience and not that of the thousands of people who have been helped by an experienced practitioner. These tales can be literally tragically misinforming.

Meditation and mindfulness

This is a common technique (comprehensively and confusingly explained everywhere on the internet) used and taught by therapists together with BREATHING to help in emotion and anxiety management. Perhaps due to conceptual blindness (see CREATIVITY AND CONCEPTUAL BLINDNESS), it is something that many children (and adults) with ASD struggle to achieve. They may perhaps in any case be 'too' mindful, given their common attention to minute detail. Once so engaged in anything, whether a video game or an insect, it can be difficult for them to extract themselves. Mindfulness can itself cause increased ANXIETY. It is best introduced as something participated in by the whole family rather than only the child with

ASD and should be introduced in a guided or facilitated manner by an adult until the child admits to spontaneously using it when needed. It should not be forced on the child and should *never involve deep breathing!* Deep breathing may worsen or even trigger a natural FIGHT–FLIGHT response when what is being sought is the opposite.

Meltdowns

Children with ASD can have meltdowns, which are far more intense and generally last longer and are distinctly different to typical tantrums. Meltdowns are generally characterised by a complete loss of control. You will probably find it very difficult, if not impossible, to rationalise with your child when they are having a meltdown and should not try as it is most likely to exacerbate the difficulty that provoked the behaviour. Over time, you will start to identify triggers or behaviours in which your child engages before a meltdown, such as pacing or more aggressive verbalising. Once you note these triggers, it is best to gently direct your child to a quiet, safe area with minimal sensory loading, as sensory overload can exacerbate a meltdown. It is important that you remember that your child is not trying to cause a scene or looking for attention (they will probably not even be aware of your presence). In fact, some children and adults who also still have them report that they can't remember the meltdown at all. Meltdowns are a response to an overloaded system that has no other way to cope. It usually arises from an ANXIETY response (FIGHT–FLIGHT), which is designed to save us when we are under serious threat. Professionals can assist you and your child in developing strategies to avoid and reduce the frequency and duration of meltdowns.

Memory

Memory is such a complex subject that people spend their lives researching only small parts. Its effects on children with ASD are significant and impact on relationships (see FACIAL BLINDNESS), LEARNING, SENSORY SENSITIVITIES and perhaps repetition (see STEREOTYPIES) and INFLEXIBILITY.

We don't just have one memory, nor are our memories located in just one place. Sensory memory, often easily overwhelmed in ASD, is that of becoming aware of what we are seeing,[58] hearing[59] and physically feeling[60] on our skin and also perhaps the other senses such as smell and taste. It recognises the perception of sensation for a fraction of a second so we can process it a little further. This may be the area that is relevant to sensory distress if there are too many sensations at once.

Short-term and working memory are terms used interchangeably by some people and as two different types by others. They allow for the brief holding in conscious mind so that we can process the information slightly further. For example, adding two figures together in our head or making a decision between which of two shirts to wear. We have to keep the information of one to add it or compare it with the other. At this point we may forget or store the information more deeply for further use. Brain scans show a lot of activity in the frontal lobe during short-term processing. This is also close to the area known for EXECUTIVE FUNCTION. In ASSESSMENTS of people with ASD, they often show difficulties in the area of working or short-term memory and this may indicate that they have difficulties with executive function. When conducting assessments, a poor result in working memory indicates to psychologists that they need to check further to work out if there are differences and difficulties with executive function. If there are, often strategies can be developed around them. The experience that many parents have of a child with ASD is that they are unable to complete a task if they are given a second instruction or if given two instructions immediately after one another. A remedy that seems to work is to 'chain' the instructions, so they are assisted to remember even an illogical progression, such as, complete your homework *and then* brush your teeth *and then* go to bed. An even better approach is to use visual reminders and teach children to keep checking back to lists.

A favourite fact about memory is that the 'telephone exchange' part of the brain is called the seahorses or hippocampi; there are two, because of their appearance. These manage the long-term storage or memory. Damage to the hippocampi can affect all of long-term memory, so that people cannot remember anything from one day to the next. They are of key importance in learning. Without the hippocampi, new memories are unable to be stored into long-term memory and concentration is adversely affected. A famous patient, known as HM (Henry Molaison),[61] had brain surgery to treat severe epilepsy. After surgery he was unable to remember events that happened since two years before the surgery and some from up to 11 years before. He could no longer store new events to his explicit or intentional memory of experiences and learning. He was able to develop new long-term procedural or physical skill-related memories, but was unable to remember learning them.

Molaison regularly completed crossword puzzles with clues that referred to his pre-surgery knowledge. For subsequent, post-surgery, details he seemed able to modify old memories with additional information.

People with ASD often have unusual ability to store information, which they may be unable to use, manipulate or access in real time. However, even after the briefest exposure to information, they may be able to retrieve it in great detail much later. This ability seems to span the senses but is most commonly seen as visual. Stephen Wiltshire is able to view the complexity of cityscapes briefly and retrieve them at will. Kim Peek, who had amazing recollection for everything that he read, as well as for facts and numbers and arithmetic ability, was the inspiration for the 1988 film *Rain Man*. (See also Mikey's story under SELECTIVE MUTISM.)

Moods

Although children who are on the autism spectrum generally struggle to recognise or express their emotional states or to understand the emotional states of others, they will still experience the full range of emotions just like everyone else. The problem is most likely that because people with ASD have EXECUTIVE FUNCTION difficulties of inadequate self-monitoring, it can be difficult for them to understand what is happening to them, and what they can do about it. Communicating their emotions is particularly challenging and even more so when in the midst of an aroused state. Like most things, early intervention is key to allowing your child to navigate through difficult times. We know that many children with ASD will also experience anxiety and/or depression. The best strategies are those that avoid triggers. As this isn't always possible, approaches such as Carol Gray's SOCIAL STORIES™ can assist, or just having multiple strategies for different contingencies developed with the child when they are calm. Trying to work with the rule of No Surprises will assist greatly but will not always prevent a situation arising. When these don't work, distraction and calming techniques are necessary and helpful.

Motor skills

Some children with ASD may have problems with some areas of motor control, making it difficult for them to engage in different, and to most people quite simple, activities. They may also be most adept at some physical abilities that are impossible for most other people. Children with ASD may exhibit many physical differences from their peers and none of these is understood at this time.[62] They may have a different style of walking or GAIT, prefer to sit with splayed legs on the floor and be hyper-flexible to the point of weak ankles and poor posture. Muscle tone may also be an issue. A favourite repetitive self-stimulatory behaviour (see STEREOTYPIES) may be 'cracking' or 'popping' joints. In children with ASD this may extend well beyond the typical knuckle-cracking to toes, shoulders, hips and even necks. While these may be quite disturbing to others, evidence for long-term harm seems difficult to find. Joint-cracking is specifically ruled out as a cause of arthritis.[63]

Fine motor skill difficulties may be best exemplified by WRITING tasks, which may be of varying difficulty to children with ASD. These challenges may limit them to slow writing or making legible writing impossible. Not one of even the most draconian of strategies has ever shown success. With assistive technology, however, writing is no longer an essential skill.

Children with ASD may also appear clumsy or struggle with coordination in physical activities. Typical gross motor problems may be in throwing and catching, often referred to as hand–eye coordination. They may also exhibit difficulties with balance. Some research has shown slower neural impulses between the motor cortex and muscles;[64]

and other research that there are differences in motor judgement as to weight, and visual cognition as to speed. On the other hand, there are successful sports people with ASD and even Olympic athletes with ASD,[65] mostly in individual participant sports such as track and field and swimming. There seem to be many issues with likely no simple solution.

While fun activities to assist with any shortcomings should always be pursued and may be with a purpose to endeavour to improve the child's skills, putting the child in front of a rugby ruck or gridiron scrimmage to force them to learn is punitive and potentially injurious. People with ASD may show interest and even excel in more solitary physical pastimes. These have included rock climbing, speed walking, sprinting and long-distance running, fencing, parachuting, swimming, tennis, table tennis, archery, luge, downhill and cross-country skiing and, no doubt, many others. People with ASD do not typically seem to be attracted to team sports to the same extent, although there are exceptions.

Mutism – see Selective mutism

N

Naughty

Children with an ASD may be labelled as 'naughty'. While it is true that all children, at some stage, are going to behave in a naughty way, often children on the autism spectrum may be called naughty when their behaviour could be more accurately described as something else and most often an ANXIETY response. Children with ASD are highly reactive to sensory input and parents quickly learn that typical reprimands or punishments or consequences will have little constructive impact. Often these types of interventions may have the opposite effect.

It is often in unfamiliar or high-stress environments that children can manifest so-called 'naughty' behaviour. Keep in mind that the underlying features of having ASD (communication and processing difficulties) are often compounded by poor sleep and heightened anxiety about unknown or new situations or environments.

When necessary try, as much as possible, to prepare your child for new experiences and changes to their routine. Planning for such events ahead of time, for example by telling a SOCIAL STORY™, reminding your child verbally, having reminders on the fridge in words and pictures and supporting them on the day, may mean that your child feels less compelled to react in a way that others may perceive as naughty. *Where possible, do not forget contingencies.* For example, the visit to relatives or a film may go wrong with any child. Having a Plan B until you are sure that your child will cope is essential. This may be a comforting toy or object or a previously identified quiet place or resource person.

When children with ASD behave in challenging ways, it is most helpful for adults to stay CALM and ensure that nothing dangerous occurs to the child or anyone else. Then try to calm your child by talking quietly, firmly guiding them to a sensorily 'quiet' or unstimulatory place, or distract them with something calming: 'Look at the waves, birds, ...' Try to avoid too much physical contact, such as hugging, unless this is a tried and trusted technique, as it may make things worse.

Neurological

Autism is a neurological condition; this means that the brains of people with ASD are different to typical people. Although presently open to debate (apparently caused by errors in measuring typical brains), areas of the brains of children with ASD were found to have greater volume.[66] This seems to begin with a spurt in growth before the age of two. The finding is helping professionals recognise the signs and diagnose ASD earlier. The frontal lobes of children with ASD have been found to have a higher density of neurons than in other children.[67] This seems due to a phenomenon called synaptic or axon pruning,[68] which in most mammals occurs between childhood and adolescence. We also believe that the areas of the brain that deal with movement and sensory information have been disrupted or are different.[69] The implication is that an ASD brain has reduced synchronisation between its elements and that this impairs different areas of functioning. This may be an explanation for the difficulty with all aspects of WRITING so often exhibited by people with ASD. It seems that they have difficulty in integrating information, seeing facts and information as distinct rather than possibly being complementary, supplementary, symbiotic, applicable or generalisable to other areas of life. For children with ASD, being polite to classmates may not translate into being polite to siblings.

O

Obsessive Compulsive Disorder (OCD)

We all have unwanted thoughts from time to time, but we can usually push them aside. People with Obsessive Compulsive Disorder (OCD) experience unwanted negative thoughts that can be constant and start to take control of their lives. People with OCD feel the need to check things repeatedly, perform certain routines or rituals repeatedly or have certain thoughts repeatedly. They are unable to control either the thoughts or the activities. Common activities include hand-washing, counting and checking to see if doors and windows are locked and lights and taps are turned off. Some may have difficulty discarding things while others may be distressed at obtaining anything new to the extent of only having limited clothes and no furniture. These activities occur to such a degree that the person's daily life is negatively affected. Often the related activities can take up many an hour each day or even every waking moment. Most typical adults with OCD realise that the behaviours do not make sense.

People with ASD who develop OCD are usually different. They will progressively develop rituals and justify them as logical and rational. This is called not having INSIGHT into the condition as compared with typical, non-ASD people who usually have great awareness of and sometimes shame at their condition. A common example of someone with ASD and OCD may be germaphobia requiring them to wear gloves, not touch anything with their hands, wear a face mask, repeatedly wash and shower throughout the day, only eat deep-fried food that they have prepared, not sit in places where others may have sat before them or even discard their clothes after a single wearing. At an extreme, this may most sadly result in the person trying to live in a hermetically sealed room, never venturing out.

For people with ASD, as for others, this may begin with a single experience or perception and grow to a disabling extent. Avoid teasing people about it or try to cajole them, as this will increase their anxiety. It is not to be taken lightly, and professional assistance is usually required (see PROFESSIONALS). In extreme cases, hospitalisation may be the only option. The therapeutic approach most regarded as effective is called EXPOSURE AND RESPONSE PREVENTION.

Organisation

Children with ASD typically have difficulty with planning, sequencing and organising. This is because people on the autism spectrum have difficulty processing information, understanding the concept of time, and also the consequences of their behaviours (also known as 'if–then' thinking, as in 'If I run onto the road, I may then be hit by a car').

This means that planning and executing everyday activities poses significant challenges. You can help your child by:

- having a routine which is followed

- ensuring that changes to the routine are planned

- using multiple strategies for changes to routine (see TRANSITIONS)

- always using SOCIAL STORIES™ or your own novel situation description

- developing a contingency 'Plan B' and, if appropriate, practising it with your child

- using verbal reminders as the occasion gets closer

- using highly visible visual and pictorial reminders *and* reminding your child of them

- practising changes, as a game, by introducing the activity or location very gradually, culminating in physically visiting/enacting the location/task (see TRANSITIONS)

- using diaries as essential tools to help, and introducing them early

- giving praise when items are remembered and completed (see TOKEN REWARD SYSTEMS).

Teaching your child to be organised early will assist them throughout their lives to have practical skills that will make them more functional and independent.

P

Pain

Pain comes into the category of SENSORY SENSITIVITIES and may present unusually in children with ASD. Some children with ASD may seem impervious to serious pain while also unduly sensitive to minor pain or even only gentle touching. For example, Jake broke his arm at school and did not tell anyone. It was only noticed some weeks later by a teacher and needed surgery to correct. On another occasion, he suffered a paper cut while looking at a comic book. His howls of distress and the damage he caused to property may have caused thoughts of a particularly violent assault rather than such a small injury. Another child called having his hair stroked bullying.

A poor response to severe pain may be problematic in that people who do not feel pain may not address injuries. A young man seriously cut his foot, severing connective tissue. Impervious to pain he merely wrapped his foot in a towel and stitched the gash himself with an ordinary needle and cotton. It was only when it became infected and he could no longer walk that the seriousness of his injury was identified. Not only did he almost lose his foot because of the infection, he needed micro-surgery and grafting to reattach the nerves and connective tissue.

Children with ASD may not be able to describe even serious pain, and this can lead to MELTDOWNS for which they may then be punished. For children with limited SPEECH or inability to express themselves, they may react to pain with distress but no explanation. Headaches, earaches, stomach aches and toothaches among others may only be indicated without words, perhaps by meltdowns. A child always placing his cheek against cool objects such as tiled floors or windows may have toothache. Another who continually holds his ears may have an earache. A child who curls into a foetal position and rocks may have a stomach ache. Regular, full medical examinations and dental check-ups for children with ASD are essential. You may have to highlight your concerns and suffer being called a neurotic parent, but a little neurotic prevention may forestall much actual distress and even challenging behaviour.

As seriously, there is deliberate self-injury (see HARM). Its prevalence in children with ASD is unknown, but clinical experience suggests that it is high and may take various forms from cutting, burning and head banging through to starving and illegal drug use. This can become a ritual or obsession and early treatment is most important. Effective therapy is that of EXPOSURE AND RESPONSE PREVENTION. Another approach used in the early stages of treatment may be Motivational Interviewing.

Parenting

Parenting can be hugely rewarding though, at times, it can seem challenging and even thankless. Parenting a child with ASD is even more complex. All parents need support and many parents with children on the spectrum report the benefits of being part of a support group. There is such a vast amount of information and opinion about ASD that it can be overwhelming. Having the right people to support you and your child is essential. This includes the PROFESSIONALS with whom you select to work. Depending on your child's needs, you may need to be involved with a range of professionals and it is important that both you and your child like them and that everyone works together. Other parents and people will often make recommendations, and the internet is filled with service providers. Be always cautious about high-priced miracle treatments for any aspect of ASD including speech, social skills and challenging behaviour. There are solutions that have been developed over many years and they can be usually quite simple and inexpensive. The most effective (and expensive but worth it) approach is, unequivocally, still EARLY INTERVENTION (EIBI) including APPLIED BEHAVIOUR ANALYSIS (ABA).

Sometimes this means that parents can forget just how important they are in the life of their child. You are super-important in your child's life and they need you to help them develop into adulthood.

Perfectionism (see also OCD)

It is often the case in ASD that rather than being an advantage, perfectionism becomes a severe and difficult-to-treat disability. It can be quite circular in that the quest for perfection is a result of fear of failure. This ANXIETY to be perfect in turn makes it more difficult to think clearly which in turn increases the difficulty of doing so. Many people with ASD-related perfectionism have above-average intelligence, but their anxiety may prevent them from performing at their desired and expected level. It can also result in inappropriate over-performance as, for example, a university student being asked to write a one-thousand-word essay, writing ten thousand words and still feeling they haven't adequately addressed the task. This may also be related to EXECUTIVE FUNCTION and the inability to know how to conclude and transition to another activity. It has been seen in children as young as five, and may be precipitated or first evident in tasks that require WRITING by hand, which children with ASD may find impossible to achieve at the level indicated by the teacher or they expect of themselves looking at their peers' work. Perfectionism may also result in PROCRASTINATION.

The best way to address this may be counterintuitive. It may need for the task to be broken down into small, achievable tasks. An alternative strategy is to artificially create much-reduced time limits, such as to write an entire essay in two hours at which time it must be presented to a teacher or parent and subsequently only have, say, one hour to revise it. Another is for the process of essay writing to be demonstrated in detail repeatedly with a narrative as to what the writer is doing but with no explanation or rationale and no questions to the person, not even a 'Do you follow?' or 'Do you understand?' All should first be demonstrated, as in the last example, by a teacher or highly proficient peer, progressively copied by the child and then gradually expanded into other areas.

Perseverative – see Stereotypies

Play (including imaginative and rough-and-tumble)

It probably does not need to be said that play is important. There are many kinds of play: alone, with siblings, with friends, with rules (sports), physical and imaginative.

Playing video games on a computer is a modern phenomenon, and its current reality of being able to play at home only less than 20 years old. Even then at first they were largely repetitive games with simple objectives and quickly became boring – although they are currently making a comeback in their original form. This form of play seems particularly attractive to children with ASD (see TECHNOLOGY) but is probably the least helpful to any area of their development and may have many quite negative consequences. These include encouraging isolation, physical inertia, perseveration, obsession (see OCD) and may cause actual physical addiction due to the stimulation of neurotransmitters. Already many adults are becoming completely isolated in their homes, living online lives to the exclusion of any external contacts. While this may seem ideal to someone with ASD, it has a worrying association with poor diet, obesity, poor health, poor hygiene and other self-care (see CARE) and increased social anxiety. One highly intelligent such person with multiple qualifications has taken eight years to progress back into, at this time, the fringes of meaningful but still unpaid work.

Active and physical play is essential for children to develop and even more for children with ASD who lack the ability to think abstractly as to how life can be beyond their direct experience. Even playing with a doll's house is an important developmental tool for both boys and girls. Pretending to walk a doll in a pram is social modelling and important. Tea parties, shops, doctors' play as well as just rolling in the grass are important. Play for any young child needs to be organised by adults when other children are not immediately available as neighbours or in nearby parks. Associating with friends may need to be scheduled into daily activities (see FRIENDS AND FRIENDSHIP). In the West, families are leading increasingly isolated lives and this does not allow a child with ASD to properly experience the range of associations and activities that are necessary for their development. Play dates are essential. Rough-and-tumble play with siblings and parents should be encouraged to a well-defined limit. This includes play fighting with proper respect of signals, and particularly tickling, which may be excruciatingly painful to a child with ASD. Physical activities to strengthen muscles and develop motor skills are essential and need to be varied to ensure the widest possible opportunities to explore their abilities.

Imaginative play may occur in children with ASD, led by others. From the age of four, concrete explanations of imaginative play (yes, it is a paradox) are necessary to help a child with ASD understand what it means. Recently, a

20-year-old with high functioning ASD remarked that his favoured computer game with knights and dragons did not need imagination. When asked, what of the designers, he was unable to appreciate that to develop a game required imagination. After about 20 minutes of denying the need for imagination he asked, 'What is it, anyway?' The complex explanation continues…

Procrastination

Procrastination is typically caused by one of three things in ASD. The first is the inability to commence a task, perhaps not quite understanding what to do or over-thinking the task as being more complex than it is and perhaps researching it so thoroughly as to cause abject confusion. The second is not being able to understand the task and perhaps feeling that they alone do not understand and, perhaps lacking the social skills, do not feel able to ask for help, even if they see other people doing so. The third may be the desire for PERFECTIONISM.

The first is likely a consequence of EXECUTIVE FUNCTION difficulties and needs to be addressed by a direct example of someone demonstrating working through a similar task, then having the child undertake the same task and then having them do progressively more tasks of increasing *difference* but not difficulty until they can do it.

The second is likely to be a consequence of both executive function and ANXIETY. It is best addressed as in the first example but may also require attention to truly appreciate your child's ability to understand. They may have deficits which may need to be properly assessed so as to have strategies developed around them (see ASSESSMENTS). This can be done by a clinical psychologist.

The third is most likely driven by anxiety and may need for the task to be broken down into small, achievable tasks and then followed through as in the first example earlier.

An additional strategy is to artificially create much-reduced time limits such as to write an entire essay in two hours at which time it must be presented to a teacher or parent and subsequently only have, say, one hour to revise it. This should again first be demonstrated as in the first example, by a teacher, copied by the child and then gradually expanded into other areas.

Professionals

Children with ASD may need almost no support, through to regular and intense support from one or many professionals. Some medical professionals can be most difficult to access and long waiting times can put off many parents. The best approach may be to identify a key person with the correct training, experience, expertise and personality, who you and your child will need to like. If they are any good, they will make this easy, and can help direct you to appropriate professional resources. It is most unlikely that any one professional will have all the attributes to help you. Don't be put off by a humble practitioner who knows their limitations.

Key professionals in ASD may be your general practitioner, a clinical psychologist or paediatrician. The paediatrician is most likely to only be seen occasionally due to their availability.

What each professional does
(in alphabetical order)
Clinical psychologist

There are many types of psychologist. The psychologists involved in treating people with disabilities and mental illness are known as clinical psychologists. They treat people of all ages and with all disabilities, but may not prescribe medication. Their training of eight or more years includes substantial practical clinical experience helping people with moderate to profound mental health problems. They provide a wide range of treatments for severe or persistent disabilities and mental illness. Clinical psychologists are also trained to take a comprehensive social, family and medical perspective. They work closely with medical professionals and allied health professionals, so suiting them to the role of case manager. Both clinical psychologists and psychiatrists help people to develop the skills needed to improve their function and to prevent ongoing problems.[70]

General practitioner

A family GP provides individual, ongoing, comprehensive health care to individuals and families in their communities. It is their job to know something about everything. All people need a GP where the provision of care is based on the relationship between them and their patients. Their medical training places general practice at the centre of an effective health care system and makes GPs suited to the role of case manager.

Occupational therapist

Occupational therapy is concerned with promoting health and wellbeing through occupation, in the broadest sense, including school and pastimes. The primary goal of occupational therapy is to enable people to participate in the activities of everyday life. Their work includes educating and involving parents, carers and others to facilitate the normal development and learning of children. They work with children, adults and communities to enhance their ability to engage in desired occupations by modifying the occupation or the environment to better support their occupational engagement. In some countries they may offer to help children with sensory sensitivities, although the benefits are unsubstantiated.[71,72]

Paediatrician

A paediatrician is a medical doctor who manages the physical, behavioural and mental health of children from birth until age 18 to 21, depending on the country in which they work. A paediatrician is trained to diagnose and treat a broad range of childhood illnesses from minor health problems to serious diseases. For the most part, they operate as expert consultants and provide direction to other health professionals such as general practitioners, clinical psychologists and allied health professionals for regular ongoing care.

Physiotherapist

Physiotherapists assess, diagnose and treat to rehabilitate disability and injury through physical exercises and help patients understand what may be wrong. Physiotherapists are experts in movement and body function who work in partnership with their patients and other health care professionals, assisting them to overcome movement limitations, which may have been present from birth, acquired through accident or injury or are the result of ageing.

Speech pathologist/therapist

Speech pathologists study, diagnose and treat communication disorders, including difficulties with speech, language, social communication, swallowing, fluency and voice. They work with people who have difficulty communicating because of developmental delays, stroke, brain injuries, learning disability, intellectual disability, cerebral palsy, dementia and hearing loss, as well as other problems that can affect speech and language.

Q

Questioning (for children)

Children (and adults) who have ASD may engage in repetitive questioning. This could be a manifestation of ECHOLALIA, or perhaps your child is unable to communicate what they want, and they could be scared or anxious. They may find comfort and reassurance in being able to talk (even if the repeated questioning is annoying). You can use SOCIAL STORIES™ to show children how people are likely to respond if they persistently ask questions. If you think ANXIETY is at the root of constant questioning, seek support from an experienced professional. If the problem is that your child is struggling to communicate, try using assistive approaches such as a story board to help direct their communication. Coloured cards can be used with children with and without speech to indicate their level of concern at any time. When teaching them how to use the cards, it will be necessary to indicate quite specifically how often they may use the 'emergency' card.

Constant questioning may also be, and commonly is, a learned habit. Children with ASD are asked many, many questions by all manner of professionals, teachers and family members. They may come to see this as normal communication and families and teachers typically respond, even if only to tell them to stop asking. Any response is a reinforcer, and the only approach is to stop any and all responses. Just be quiet, as difficult as that may be. You may choose a gentle comforting hand on an arm or leg, but nothing more than this is appropriate as it too may come to reinforce the unwanted behaviour.

Questioning (for parents)

In our culture, it is common to ask questions to make small talk, to obtain ideas and have people think about events (Socratic questioning) and even ask complex rhetorical questions where no response is expected. None of these will work with children on the spectrum. *Questions should be simple and concrete.* This cannot be sufficiently emphasised, and not sticking to this rule may cause unbelievable ANXIETY and even MELTDOWNS. Even asking 'How was school?' or 'What did you do at school?' may cause great confusion and distress. If one is literal, how is it possible to answer such a question? For a literal child they would need to describe every minute of their school day, and they may not remember. They will wish to please you by answering but be so confused as to become distressed. They may even answer 'I don't know', only to be told authoritatively by their loving, knowledgeable parent 'But, you must know!'

One young child always had meltdowns when fetched from school by his mother. He was also collected by Dad and Grandmother on other days with no problems. Recordings by the adults from when the child entered the car immediately clarified the problem. Mum was a highly sociable and gregarious person who loved chatting and would, naturally, ask lots of questions about school and friends. Dad was quite taciturn and would just grunt a greeting and then be silent, with the whole trip in seemingly companionable silence. Grandma would say a cheery 'hello', provide the child a snack and then tell the child what she, Grandma, had been doing, so that there was no requirement for the child to say anything. Mum, with difficulty, learned, after greeting, to be quiet for a while and then ask concrete questions, such as 'Who did you play with at first break?', allow a further period of quiet and then describe her day, perhaps with a subsequent question 'Who did you sit next to in art?' This strategy solved the problem and made life much easier all around. It had a secondary purpose of teaching the child, by example, how to make conversation.

With PROFESSIONALS, as parents you may find that you have a lot of questions early on and progressively about your child, such as 'Is this typical?' and 'What do I do about…?' It is normal and helpful that you ask questions as you will be the one who puts plans into action. When you take your child to see professionals, it is important for you to understand what is going on.

Quirky (see also Idiosyncrasies)

The major similarity of all children with ASD is that they are all different and quirky. It can be a delightful attribute, enjoyable eccentricity or annoying aspect of their behaviour. Children with ASD are individuals with unique personalities and interests. Even those with severe intellectual impairments are, if we take the time to discover, great personalities looking for opportunities to show their qualities. To some parents, this may appear a particularly optimistic view and some poor parents may be too exhausted to be able to see these qualities. Some children may also hide their qualities behind their highly distressing behaviour. With help, most children and parents can come to enjoy their time together.

R

Reading

Children with ASD can have great difficulty with language, and English in particular. Native English speakers on the spectrum have been known to exhibit greater skill and comfort with German and Japanese languages. While the difficulties that even some high functioning children have with spoken language may be obvious, the difficulty they have with reading is much less understood and may not be at all apparent.

Children with ASD seem to read and absorb the information in one of three ways, all of which may be unhelpful to a greater or lesser degree. They have great difficulty changing their style, as they do with all their other activities. This can be hidden by, for many, an apparent love of reading and seeming great desire to do so. They can read extensively and quickly but may understand only a little. Reading is a repetitive behaviour such as self-stimulatory (see STEREOTYPIES) behaviours that children may find calming, as many are obviously relaxed when they read. Some find that the practical act of having a book between them and others reduces anxiety. It is worth being aware that many intellectually impaired children enjoy just turning the pages in books. While this used to be thought of as just copying other people's behaviour, this page-turning seems to continue unabated notwithstanding most people now visibly using tablets and computers. There appears to be no research on additional benefit from turning pages.

Some children with ASD, firstly, seem to skim read. They appear to only read a few words from each sentence and seem disinclined to reread the passage if they do not understand what they have read. This can occur throughout their lives but is typically observed in children, teens and young adults at university. This may have something to do with the finite capacity of their working MEMORY. They may also have this difficulty if they are reading or trying to copy words projected or written onto a screen or board. When they copy words onto a page or, for that matter, type on a laptop, they appear to be unable to accurately track from left to right. Their reading skips from a word in a line to the line below and sometimes skips whole lines altogether. In this case, the difficulty may be increased by WRITING difficulties which are most likely a problem with the way their brain works rather than how their wrists or fingers do (see MOTOR SKILLS).

A second way they seem to read is to read each single *line* as a whole with an imaginary full-stop at the end of each line, without thought of context and without simultaneous understanding. For children who do this voluntarily, it seems to have a calming effect. When doing so for school work, though, it only allows the most rudimentary understanding of what they are reading and may impede their learning and knowledge development.

The third way they seem to read is to read each *sentence* alone and out of context without any real processing. When asked immediately, they may be able to repeat a few words and the superficial meaning but, again, there is no proper understanding. This also seems to have something to do with an overloaded working memory.

There are simple strategies to help address these issues. These include: larger type; holding a ruler under the line being read and moving it down the page; reading out loud with an adult encouraging understanding of meaning by *telling and not asking*; and practising reading each syllable in time with a slow-beating metronome to learn an appropriate reading speed. However, while children are learning to read to a beat, due to their concentration on the metronome they may be unable to concentrate on content so this is a multistage stage process.

Text-to-word software should only be used with headphones and with the child following the words heard on the screen in front of them. They should never be used while engaged in another activity as poor habits will be learned.

Refusal

Most common in children with ASD is school refusal. They may, however, refuse to participate in any activities and sometimes activities they may have enjoyed only a day before. Refusal seems to be of two types: the first is to stop them doing something they enjoy; and the second is to have them do something which they perhaps don't want to do.

There are reasons that seem to have changed over time. These reasons are parallel with the development of electronic games (see TECHNOLOGY) has been an increase in perseveration (see OCD, ROUTINES), perhaps the comfort and lack of personal or social demands and the CALM and minimisation of ANXIETY that computer games engender. There are also addictive qualities of games,[73] which may be quite neurological if theories about the effects of the production of dopamine continue to be verified. Note that these addictive elements are deliberately built into some game designs to encourage their use in the same way as reinforcement is built into gambling technology. A teenager with ASD was recently reported to have spent ten thousand dollars in a month on 'free' computer games. These games seem to 'stall' or 'lock' children into repetitive activities for which, according to the formal diagnosis, they have an intrinsic inclination. As a result, any efforts to extract children from these and transition them to another activity can be extremely difficult and result in unwanted BEHAVIOUR. Taking a child away from a situation of great comfort to them needs a structured approach and the learning of better and new habits. (See also TOKEN REWARD SYSTEMS.)

The other aspect of refusal to participate can be a result of having no idea and considerable anxiety about what it is that they are expected to do, or having previously had a bad similar experience. SOCIAL STORIES™ and contingency plans are an important approach to correcting this.

SCHOOL refusal can be so complex as to necessitate many approaches and that of EIBI–ABA and calming, anxiety reduction and emotional regulation may need to be incorporated into a comprehensive strategy (see calm, anxiety, EMOTIONS AND REGULATION). From the understanding that is obtained through ABA, a moment-by-moment re-entry to school should be carefully planned and implemented with No Surprises, Keep It Calm, Keep It Simple and No Failures as the overriding policy.

Regression

This refers to a reversal of behaviour gains that may be seen in children with ASD at any time as they develop. This can occur in relation to family dislocation, parental distress, bullying or many other causes. It should be taken seriously and investigated with a professional as soon as possible. The most common areas to show regression are speech, movement and development more generally, especially in social domains.

A second meaning is that of Regressive-type Autism, which refers to a third type of autism (the others are *with* and *without* normal speech development), where children are seen to develop typically but then before the age of two (usually) they rapidly are discerned to lose the skills they have already acquired (speech, social skills, movement/coordination) and become more isolated with increased self-stimulatory behaviour (see STEREOTYPIES). Research has shown that about one quarter of children on the autism spectrum have been thought to develop in this way.[74] This is a contentious subject and the latest diagnostic manual excludes this presentation. It is also associated with the discredited and debarred English doctor Andrew Wakefield, who wrongly attributed ASD to children's vaccinations.[75,76]

Notwithstanding, many parents and clinicians continue to report it.

A reasonable theory is that many parents are skilled at interpreting their infants' early efforts at speech. As speech becomes more obvious, the early gains plateau and expected progress stalls. Whether this is what occurs in children who exhibit this type of ASD is only conjecture. It can be as distressing to parents as an early diagnosis and can leave them with thoughts as to what they may have done wrongly. This needs to be dispelled. There is no evidence of any parental involvement in causing most types of autism. Only in very occasional cases of violence against infants are some ASD-like symptoms apparent.

Reinforcement

Reinforcement refers to anything that increases the behaviour, whether intended, desired or not. Research shows that if we receive recognition, punishment, praise or a positive or negative reward, all referred to as reinforcement, following a behaviour, we are much more likely to again engage in this behaviour. The key to successful reinforcement is that we only reinforce desired behaviour.[77] When we punish unwanted behaviour, this is also a reinforcer, and we are likely to see the unwanted behaviour repeated. Any action following a behaviour can be a reinforcer, even ringing a bell, for example, properly called Classical Conditioning.[78,79] Sometimes opportunities for appropriate reinforcement of desired behaviour can be brief, such as the CALM after MELTDOWNS or quiet at the dinner table. It is so much easier to respond to things that upset us as adults that we forget this may have the opposite effect to that intended.

Structured approaches to reinforcement are most important and the TOKEN REWARD SYSTEMS are probably the best known and most effective of these.

Briefly, the child should have visual and calm verbal reminders of desired behaviour and the outcomes of that. They should receive token rewards in a systematic approach specifically designed for their age and ability.

Some examples of reinforcers include:

- praise (high-fives, hugs, certificates)

- desired objects (small, inexpensive and behaviour-appropriate, e.g. stickers)

- free time or structured activity (most children with ASD prefer structured time as they have difficulty initiating behaviour)

- preferred activities (technology, with great care and with strict time limits attached)

- privileges (sitting in a preferred place, choosing the TV channel).

Repetitive – see Stereotypies

Restraining
Children (and adults) with autism sometimes exhibit behaviours that are unacceptably unsafe for them and

you and beyond your (and their) control (see HARM). Restraining, however, is a controversial subject.

Simply, if any child (or adult) is having a meltdown, the recommended intervention is to *do nothing* at all, unless absolutely necessary for their safety. That is, ignore the behaviour by not looking at, talking to or touching the child or adult, except to the extent essential for safety.

Over time, not intervening will help to reduce the meltdowns, because the child no longer receives attention nor any reinforcement for their behaviour.

If the behaviour occurs *more than once*, seek professional assistance. If there is a particular pattern that occurs, note the specifics. They may be important. Consider if any of the behaviours appear protective or indicate physical discomfort (see PAIN).

There are some behaviours that cannot be ignored. For example, a meltdown that lasts all day and involves violence against self or others, including breaking things. For small children, we can intervene physically to stop the behaviour. When they grow, physical intervention is no longer an option. The time to intervene is early (see EARLY INTERVENTION).

Restraints are usually advocated where the behaviour puts the person with ASD and others at risk of harm. The behaviour is assaultive! The person is trying to hurt others or themselves and is so out of control that harm is likely. It is behaviour that in an adult would or should result in police attendance.

What can you do?
Do nothing

Having already tried talking calmly, preferably not shouting and, avoiding physically restraining the child, if this 'strategy' has not worked, stop. Do not talk to the child, do not look at them directly, although you should observe them indirectly and only touch them to guide them for safety. This will avoid exacerbating the meltdown.

If you are being attacked directly, defend yourself with blocking. If this behaviour is frequently necessary, attending a non-violent self-defence or crisis intervention programme is recommended.

Resist restraining your child

Some children like being held, finding it comforting and will develop meltdowns in order to be restrained. However, it perversely teaches children to have meltdowns so as not to have to self-regulate and to be violent to obtain succour.

Go to a safe place

Sometimes your presence may precipitate a meltdown and cause it to continue. If you can observe the person from outside a room, in safety, this is best. If it is a regular occurrence you may need a lockable room where you can safely phone for assistance. If the child settles, even if they are sobbing quietly, leave them for a further period before going to them. If there is any escalation, leave and get help.

If they become peaceful, continue as if nothing has happened

Much later, when they have become truly calm, instruct them *calmly, simply, concisely* and *directly*, preferably in words previously used to describe your desired behaviour for them, for example, using Carol Gray's SOCIAL STORIES™. For non-verbal or hearing impaired children use picture stories *later*. Remain calm and act deliberately even if you are concerned. Do not show distress. While it is unlikely that the child will perceive your distress (see THEORY OF MIND), you can give yourself time out later.

Obtain help

If you know that one person can usually calm the child, have them accessible as far as possible. Watch what they do and practise copying them, exactly. If they are available, leave them to do what they do and provide support, even if you are Mum or Dad and the person is a neighbour.

Involve the police

If the child is violent and not improving, call the police. This is appropriate. Many parents may see this as a step too far until the child is an uncontrollable teen or adult when the action has to be taken with far more serious consequences.

Even a single episode of violence, even if it is managed, should result in a conversation with local police and development of a crisis plan. They should meet with your child and everyone should know what their respective roles are. Explain to the police about your child, about ASD, and about what you would *prefer* them to do if you called in a crisis. Understand that when they become involved they have laws, rules and regulations that they have to follow and that they will not voluntarily place themselves in danger. Their presence may be enough to defuse the situation. If your child with autism needs to be transferred to a hospital, the police or an ambulance will do this. Never drive with a violent child in your car.

When you are alone in your 'safe' room, call the police, explain the situation, and what you would like for them to do. They will tell you what they can and cannot do. Wait for them to arrive. Allow them to deal with your child and do not intervene. The police may be able to calm the situation enough so they can leave and all will be well. If you need to talk to them, do so when your child is calm and out of earshot.

Do not warn or threaten that you will call the police. Previously, you will have already advised that violent behaviour *will* lead to the police coming to the home.

Over time the child needs to be able to recognise and communicate distress without violence. Discuss with your trusted PROFESSIONALS how to achieve this without outside intervention. By teaching the child to recognise their distress and to tell someone, even by pointing to a part of their body and perhaps indicating by gestures or with pre-prepared pictures, the cause or desired remedy can usually be achieved. Regularly and when calm, rehearse relaxation strategies: sorting cards or blocks, flicking through pages in a book, other simple repetitive activities, listening to music, going to a quiet and calming place are all useful. Deep breathing, computer games, food and rewards are not usually appropriate.[80]

Rituals

Ritualised behaviour is common to all children who may prefer, for example, being read to in bed before sleep or even saying a prayer before bed, without which they will not sleep. All people seem to have some of these, and some may be seen as superstitions or even as silly by the person themselves, such as an adult having a toy in bed. We may feel unease if we are prevented from sitting in our usual seat or forced to take a detour by road works. If these repeated behaviours have no direct positive or negative implications and cause anxiety to vary, they have probably shifted from being useful to habitual to ritual, that is, a sequence of activities performed in a place according to a set sequence with no obvious utility beyond us not having to think about them. Most typically the automated use of a motor vehicle, to the point of forgetting where we were going or being unable to remember in detail how we arrived, is one such example. We probably spare brain capacity for novel tasks by automating those which are frequently repeated. If there are no negative implications, they may not be worth changing.

Children with ASD quite often develop these and exhibit them to a greater and perhaps more extreme extent. They may acquire an extensive pattern which may grow to hours of different behaviours and can include making noise, different gestures, pacing, sorting or disturbing objects and can distort into compulsions (behaviour) and obsessions (thoughts) that may result in a perception of threat, harm or directly cause severe anxiety if not followed. Early professional assistance should be sought for this as it may develop into OBSESSIVE COMPULSIVE DISORDER, a most debilitating condition if left to do so.

Routines

While all children benefit from having predictable routines in their lives, children with ASD are especially in need of routines given how unpredictable, frightening and confusing the world can seem to them. Children who are on the autism spectrum will often naturally adapt to an appropriate routine. To them, it is usually gratifying and comforting to have this sense of order, though it is necessary to monitor lest it becomes part of an obsession or ritual, which can be problematic when there are the inevitable changes to a routine. As your child develops and the complexities of life increase, planning will become increasingly important and children may be inclined to steadfastly cling to old routines. Preparing your child for changes to a routine, no matter how big or small, is essential to minimising their anxiety. (See also TRANSITIONS.)

S

School

Each day at school for a child with ASD can be a new challenge with quite unexpected, unpredictable and, therefore, disconcerting and distressing occurrences. This may be different sounds, sights, patterns, children, teachers, classes or an almost infinite range of different experiences, people and interactions. Children on the spectrum will usually try to control their environment and make order from the chaos. Depending on their levels of distress, this may range from merely appearing bossy to becoming aggressive if their tolerance is exhausted.

To assist children with ASD and their teachers and parents, a detailed structured learning and behaviour plan needs to be developed. It is important that this plan is comprehensive, and it must be developed around the child and not the context, while being context-specific; the support needed by the child will most likely be different in a language lesson compared with a mathematics lesson. Some children with ASD who are quite intelligent may be unable to concentrate for more than 30 minutes without a break. They will need to have such a break scheduled with whatever supports may be necessary. They may be unable to tolerate the noise of the cooling fan in the data projector. This has happened quite often, in case you were wondering. How then will information be made available to them? They may have difficulty in organising their books, their work station or any other aspect, and such support will again need to be stipulated and may include a colour-coded timetable and colour coding of associated books and stationery. My general and preferred recommendation is a plan for every 15 to 30 minutes of each school day, for the entire time awake each day, and initiated before the commencement of term and reviewed between teachers, parents and child, depending on age, every four weeks of term.[81]

Selective mutism

Selective mutism may be related to underlying social anxiety, although it may be quite personal as in the examples that follow. This could be due to struggles with understanding social communication, which can trigger fear of not being able to respond appropriately or in a way that can be understood by others. It can also just be a dislike of hearing their own voice, a dislike of their voice's tone, an inability to find words to properly express their thoughts or thinking that they cannot do so as quickly as others. They may think they are dumb, or it could just be a game they choose to play because they attract attention and usually a great deal of support and helpful understanding. Some examples from clients follow.

A 14-year-old boy with ASD had never spoken. As a child, Mikey had never appeared to develop language.

The family had accommodated it and so had his schools. His behaviour was always good (perhaps not such a good thing in that he avoided any attention, as a result). Mikey had performed reasonably to his assumed ability at a special school, developing some skills in mathematics and science but was thought to have done so to a much lesser extent in English. Expectations were low as he was prone to frequent self-stimulatory behaviours (see STEREOTYPIES), mostly flapping, flicking and rocking. At home Mikey would sit with the family but not engage. While the family watched TV, he would usually sit and flick through classic books such as *Shakespeare's Complete Works*, inherited by the family from his grandfather. This was thought to be calming for him (see CALM), and he was left to do so.

One evening the family were sitting watching TV when their concentration was disturbed by the soft but persistent sound of a formal speech, which seemed to be from a drama or the reciting of poetry. Dad went from room to room and even outside thinking it was a radio or even an emergency vehicle radio. It took some moments until Mikey's sister exclaimed: 'He's speaking!' Not only was he speaking, it transpired that he had memorised long passages of many of the classical works that he appeared to have enjoyed flicking through. These included the complete works of Shakespeare, *War and Peace* and a number of others. With the assistance of a speech therapist he developed his speaking skills and with a massive effort from him and on the part of teachers and his family, he graduated from secondary school at the appropriate age with a previously unthought-of pass and went on to university to study chemistry. He disclosed that he had previously practised his speech in bed at night but didn't want to do so aloud until he 'had it right'.

In another instance a middle-aged married woman and mother was quite unable to speak in front of extended family and close friends and yet worked in retail with no difficulty, speaking to customers and colleagues and even being promoted to a supervisory position.

Another young man, according to him, 'hid' his voice until adulthood as he didn't like its tone.

Selective mutism (sometimes just called mutism) is complex and likely an anxiety-related disorder where children refuse to speak at all or will speak to a restricted number of specific people, often in specific settings. Mutism normally presents in social settings, often at school. Children are usually diagnosed with this condition between the ages of three and eight years old and parents and friends will often note that the child was extremely shy prior to the formal diagnosis being made. A better prognosis is associated with early diagnosis and intervention. As a parent, the best thing you can do is to access adequate professional support (see PROFESSIONALS) and to acknowledge and normalise your child's anxiety and worries (for example, by saying, 'I know you're scared') but to also remember to praise them for their accomplishments. Always seek out opportunities to praise and reward good behaviour to boost your child's sense of self. Focusing on your child having decided to stop speaking may make the behaviour even more anxiety-provoking to your child and could make the mutism more entrenched.

Self-care – see Care

Self-harm – see Harm and Pain

Self-stimulatory – see Stereotypies

Sensory sensitivities (see also Pain)

Children with ASD are often noted for their acute hearing and may even be commented upon as having 'elephants' ears' (auditory sensitivity) and 'eagles' eyes' (visual sensitivity). They are less often described as having a 'dog's nose' (olfactory sensitivity), a 'super taster's taste' (a real term for gustatory sensitivity) or a 'safe-cracker's nano-touch' (tactile sensitivity). Even though few children would recognise it in themselves or be aware of it as it is occurring, they often exhibit an 'unconscious threat-hypersensitivity', and yet they can have all of these to a greater or lesser extent. There are also likely to be specific variations of these, for example: visually, sensitivity to bright or flashing lights or darkness; tactilely, a desire for being firmly held or swaddled, with an aversion to soft touch or having hair brushed. It can include insistence on fans all year around but an intolerance of air conditioning. A child may enjoy the sensation of a hair dryer being used but be unable to tolerate the sound of a vacuum cleaner. To food, add its texture, and its appearance including the appearance of its texture (Yes! Lumps are usually out, even if in ice cream and even if they dissolve) and add its colour to its taste and the possibilities for distress about food multiply exponentially. These can all be triggers for anxiety-related FIGHT–FLIGHT and consequent challenging BEHAVIOUR.

We can spend much time attempting to understand them, and perhaps eventually so doing. For more immediate benefit, avoid the contexts where these occur, provide workarounds, extend similarities beyond logic, and provide mechanical aids such as: sunglasses or plain glass spectacles with blinkers (minimising peripheral vision); ear muffs or noise-cancelling headphones; gloves and long-sleeved tops and bottoms; slippers instead of shoes or bare feet. Your creativity knows no bounds in the quest for sensitivity solutions. Most children do experience either decreasing sensitivity or a greater accommodation of the different sensations as they get older. While there are many programmes and clinicians to ostensibly help, and numerous strategies such as using a hairbrush on arms and getting children gradually accustomed to vacuum cleaners, these may and likely will all fall apart in your home or a different context.

Another element to the sensory sensitivities of people with ASD is the quite incredible attribute of synaesthesia, where a sensory stimulation, say of smell, invokes a colour or a musical note a particular visual sensation or taste. This appears to be present in people with ASD and can add to the confusion and distress that children may experience. They may cover their eyes but the sensation may be more difficult to deal with if the cause of their distress is auditory.

Silent films

Silent films is a fun technique for teaching children from about three years about attention to faces and body language, non-verbal communication, contexts and emotions. Some animated films can be a good start. The idea is to watch a new film with the sound off for, to begin with, say five minutes. Each family member guesses as to what is happening and explains their reasons for their guesses. The sound is then turned on and the part of the film again watched to see who was closest. The length of time can be increased gradually and the film's complexity extended to actual dramas. Most of the big-budget clash of machines or robots films are not as useful. It is also important to preview the film to ensure that the actors have not had Botox injections which prevents their faces from exhibiting natural expression. Best are the pre-2000s classics.

Films with lots of dialogue can become quite challenging and useful in real life. Children with ASD who have played this game for some years become quite adept at reading expressions and emotions and much more socially adept than those who do not practise. Even children without speech develop much greater assurance, perhaps through the experience and having other family members describe their take of a particular scene.

Sleep

Everyone needs sleep and a sleep routine. Children need much more sleep than adults. Primary school children should have at least ten hours per day and high school teens nine hours per day. This usually means getting ready for and being in bed some reasonable time before the anticipated start of sleep.

Dinner needs to be a good while before sleep, so that children do not go to bed and lie down straight away, which may make them feel unwell. All self-stimulatory activities, technology, TV, rough-and-tumble, should stop at least an hour before bed. Chores can be relaxing, and scheduling these with visible visual prompts is important for children with ASD.

Most children, including those with ASD, will have night terrors at some time.[82,83] These are common and typically occur when children are deeply asleep. Checking to see they are safe is important. Waking them only to try to get them back to sleep can be disruptive and deeply distressing to them. Unlike night*mares*, which are dreams during REM sleep and often remembered, children will not have any memory of a night *terror*, because they were in deep sleep and there are no mental images to recall. During night terrors, a child may suddenly sit upright in bed and shout out or scream in distress. Their breathing and heart rates might be faster; they may sweat, lash out and act upset and scared. Usually, after a few minutes, the child will simply calm down and continue to sleep. The only need of intervention is to ensure they remain safe. As said, try not to wake them as this will be disruptive to their sleep and waking from deep sleep can be quite disturbing. If you have ever been jarred out of deep sleep by a disturbance, you will know this yourself.

Anxiety, as many adults have experienced, can affect sleep. There is a neurological reason involving the production of cortisol in our adrenal glands,[84,85] which is part of our FIGHT–FLIGHT response and among other things may keep us awake or affect the quality of sleep. Children with ASD have *dis*similar cortisol times and rates of production compared with typical children. Most people experience a doubling of their cortisol levels on waking, which allows them to prepare for their day. They also exhibit aroused levels at times of changing activities.

Social skills

The difficulties people with ASD experience and suffer with their social skills is one of the diagnostic criteria for ASD. It is one of the many observational criteria; we observe it in people with ASD, and therefore it is in the criteria. What causes it is not understood, and because social interactions are so complicated it is very difficult to research. Lots of research of mental conditions can only investigate tiny aspects, given the limited tools we have available. What is often forgotten about the 'diagnostic criteria' is that they are equally there to encourage research.

A great deal of effort is made to help children with ASD become socially adept, with little evidence that it works. There are few rigorous independent evaluations of the many and often costly programmes that are on offer. Most of these fail through the sheer dynamism of social engagement. What we appropriately do as children is not necessarily appropriate as teens or as adults. What is appropriate at home isn't necessarily appropriate at school, work or in church. What is appropriate with men may not be appropriate with women. What a child believes to be friendly, another may perceive as abusive; and what they may discern as teasing or bullying attention may be kindness. While enjoying casual sport and participating in a level of physical activity, perhaps cross-country running, playing in teams with or against others may be complicated by an inability to either grasp the rules of the game or an insistence that, even during social play, rules be strictly enforced. One child insisted on passing a football to the opposing team, because he had been taught to share. When told by a well-meaning teacher that this was inappropriate, he became a horror towards his siblings and cousins. This took months to resolve. Children may seek to impose rules that suit them but are detrimental to others. They may even insist on being given others' food or Pokémon cards, for example, and be accused of bullying.

Similarly, adults with ASD may find working in groups or on committees difficult; while they can be extremely hard-working and knowledgeable participants, they may not understand the dynamic fluidity ranging between formal and informal processes, seeking to impose formality on casual interactions or possibly providing casual or inappropriate input at times of formality. Usually they are not adept people managers. A quite depressed man was known as a joker and frequently played childish tricks on colleagues at work, eventually losing his job for doing so.

Contrary to superficial explanations, we don't have a 'social lobe' in our brain. We do, however, have areas for recognising patterns of behaviour and one area specialised for facial recognition (see FACIAL BLINDNESS).

MEMORY is located in many areas and one of its key components, the hippocampi, are located in the frontal lobe, thought to be the location of many ASD-related difficulties. These include black-and-white or dichotomous thinking, repetition and perseveration, and difficulties with different types of FLUID REASONING. Social engagement may also be affected by the amygdala, shown to play a key role in the processing of emotions. In children (also adults and animals), this brain structure is linked to fear responses and pleasure (see FIGHT–FLIGHT). In testing, children with ASD show that these areas may be differently developed. Under its different sections, this book covers the difficulties with EMOTIONS AND REGULATION, FRIENDS AND FRIENDSHIP, CREATIVITY AND CONCEPTUAL BLINDNESS and the many aspects of social appropriateness.

Under LANGUAGE there are descriptions of some related difficulties that interfere in the ability to appreciate and navigate the complexity of human interactions. Under ANIMALS there is comment as to why children with ASD may find animals to be so much easier as objects for friendship. Under FACIAL BLINDNESS are some other clues to their social challenges. SELECTIVE MUTISM describes a possible intermediate aspect of ASD where communication abilities exist but are, possibly linked to ANXIETY, not expressed.

SOCIAL STORIES™, discussed in the next section, are one of the most helpful strategies and have been developed and used for many years. You can make up your own, and it will be helpful to record them in a journal, so that other adults in your child's life can develop an understanding of the approach and what you are focusing on. Indicative of the complexity of social situations, the book by Carol Gray[86] contains 158 examples of social stories and is by no means exhaustive.

Social Stories™

Social Stories™ are short visual or spoken stories that are used to describe social situations. They break down individual potentially challenging social situations into understandable elements, anticipating the particular difficulties that may be experienced by someone with ASD. They are highly descriptive to help the child with ASD know what to expect in a novel situation. The stories as described by the author, Carol Gray, as covering who, what, when, where, and why of social situations through the use of visuals and text. Social

Stories™ are also used to teach particular social skills, such as greeting or understanding that a restaurant is different to a dinner table and how behaviour should be modified accordingly. They typically cover taking another person's point of view (a difficult construction for people with ASD), understanding rules, routines, situations, upcoming events and abstract concepts, and understanding expectations.

Another way to describe Social Stories™ could be risk management or contingency planning. It is always a good idea to have additional strategies available in case the first doesn't work.

Social Stories™ were developed to help people with ASD better understand social situations and interpersonal communication, so that they can interact in an effective and appropriate manner. While originally designed for high functioning people with basic communication skills, they have also shown merit for some people with poor communication skills and low-level functioning. Live social modelling (learning) with prompting and simple explanations may be more effective for some of these children, though.

Special interests

This is the term given to particular interests in which children (and adults) with ASD become particularly invested, to an unusual extent. This may become obsessive in that they may want to know or do everything possible related to their interest and to the exclusion of other activities. Special interests seem not to be as directly related to feelings of ANXIETY as they are in OCD, in that they are typically a source of obvious pleasure and, depending on their nature, may be used constructively in TOKEN REWARD SYSTEMS.

Typical interests for young children with ASD may be insects, dinosaurs, cars, Lego, trains and collections of toys and dolls. While physical activities such as dancing for both boys and girls may also be a focus, most children with ASD do not naturally gravitate towards physical activities as they may be averse to getting hot, for example (see SENSORY SENSITIVITIES and PAIN). Children may evince great interest in a subject but when you assist or encourage them they lose interest. Recently a mother bought her daughter a ferret as the girl had been watching videos of ferrets, reading about them and talking about them at length. The child's reaction to the animal was one of horror. After all, ferrets are quite unpredictable and seldom do what their owners want although they can apparently be trained.

Speech (see also Language)

Children with ASD may have no speech, may have sounds (speech apraxia/alalia), may have speech ability but be selectively mute (see SELECTIVE MUTISM), may have speech but it may not be understandable (speech dyspraxia/ dyslalia), may have highly complex speech, may have speech without punctuation, may speak without having a grammatical object in mind, may speak literally, may have unusual patterns, accents, tone (prosody) and other noticeable differences including ECHOLALIA and palilalia (self-echoing). All of these conditions can benefit from the assistance of a speech pathologist. Most if not all children can be assisted to learn to communicate basic needs and follow simple directions at the very least, and usually more.

Children with ASD appear to acquire speech in a quite different way to their peers, perhaps as a result of different ways of hearing or giving attention to other people (see SOCIAL SKILLS, FACIAL BLINDNESS).

While speaking may occur early, it is also often delayed; and in both cases those acquiring speech spontaneously, compared with those who don't speak, often learn to speak in phrases without having first learned words. They learn these phrases from hearing their parents and teachers and from TV or games. Some are quite adept at stringing these together to make sentences of apparent meaning and using quite advanced words. However, the entire sentence may not make great sense when considered in detail. They may use phrases inappropriately in conjunction with correct responses, having heard them in different contexts (a parent swearing at home or an announcement at an airport). They may become adept at parroting. This can also be the case with READING.

Correcting of speech difficulties should only be pursued to the point where it doesn't cause anxiety. Insisting on difficult word use or pronunciation may cause such anxiety as to trigger mutism. It may also cause parroting of the demonstrated exaggerated pronunciation, such as a very sibilant 'S' or forced staccato 'T'.

Stereotypies

The criterion 'B' of the *Diagnostic and Statistical Manual of Mental Disorders, DSM-5* for Autism Spectrum Disorder is, to paraphrase, limited and repetitive behaviours, interests and activities. Although not in the formal diagnosis, most people with ASD who can articulate their thoughts also report that they have repetitive thoughts and often repetitive dreams. This last, though, seems common in many people, not only those with ASD. A formal diagnosis requires two from a list of presentations for this criterion to be met. It includes a wide breadth of behaviours which are called many different things and often with considerable overlap.

The first of these behaviours or presentations listed to meet diagnostic criteria is 'stereotyped or repetitive' physical movements, including where it may include objects or repetitive, sometimes called perseverative or even pressured, speech. The term perseveration is also most usually used in relation to persistent thoughts both in ASD and other areas of psychology. The range included here may be the lining up, building into long towers or sorting into colours of Lego blocks. It may also include flapping, flicking, rocking or spinning, called variously stereotypies, self-stimulatory or stimming. Vocally the behaviour may be repetitive sounds, phrases, ECHOLALIA or repeated recitation of facts (numbers) or lengthy poems or quotes. The criteria do not specify whether these are the result or cause of anxiety nor whether pleasing or calming. At times in the same child, they may appear to flap due to anxiety indicating distress, a self-regulation strategy to address anxiety or just because they seem to enjoy it. Children may often exhibit stereotypy in relation to external activities such as a washing machine or other motorised appliance. They will quite often repeatedly stop their actions to press close to the appliance as if listening intently, step back and repeat their behaviours with total self-absorption. As trying to remove them may cause a meltdown, this suggests that it is an enjoyable activity. On other occasions they will demonstrate the behaviour with obvious indications of distress.

The second group of behaviours or conduct goes to INFLEXIBILITY or insistence on routines, habits or rituals that may also be either or both verbal or non-verbal. This may be as simple as insisting on travelling the same way to work each day *and* becoming distressed if this is not possible. It may be indicated by particularly repetitive work such as on an assembly line, again though, by definition, causing distress if not possible. It may include talking or not talking in specific contexts such as while driving. Persistent and sometimes extremes of thought such as particular beliefs, including in scientific and non-scientific facts, as well as conviction about conspiracies are quite common. Once a particular view is reached it is most difficult to change, no matter the evidence provided. People with ASD often have difficulty with imagining anything outside their personal experience (see CREATIVITY AND CONCEPTUAL BLINDNESS) so something that to them appears impossible may be rejected out of hand. So too, though, may advances in technology and medicine. Inflexibility may include patterns of speech, phrases, words that don't make sense in context, non-words used repeatedly in sentences and sounds used in patterns. Some of these may appear to almost be verbal TICS. Children may become most distraught at any changes, including if their favoured breakfast isn't available (see TRANSITIONS). Another area that has relevance is the almost obsessional (see OCD) nature of many of these and how they can significantly impact on the enjoyment of life, mostly when for some reason they may not be possible or available. The difference between many 'obsessional' routines, habits or rituals in ASD compared with OCD is that they are not usually distressing to people with ASD. This is not the same as phobias, which may give rise to avoidance obsessions and are always distressing as they cause deep anxiety.

The third group of conducts is that of extreme limitation in interest or focus, including attention to minutiae well beyond the ability of most people. This may include gifted academics with life-long attention to extremely narrow fields of study, year after year, and being unconcerned at persistently replicating research to expand their understanding. Many breakthroughs in science have been achieved by people with ASD due to this ability for narrow focus.

Unfortunately, this may also limit the ability of such people to engage fully in society due to their extremely limited areas of interest. A fixed interest on cricket statistics may not make for lively conversation at a dinner party, which most people with ASD would highly dislike. Children with ASD are notorious for hiding in their rooms during birthday parties because their guests may not share their limited interests or due to disinterest in social activities (see SOCIAL SKILLS).

For children, these limited interests are often referred to as 'special' but are nonetheless quite restricted, usually to one or two at any one time. It may be space and dinosaurs or wheels and insects. Other limited interests in children have included Harry Potter, Hello Kitty, Manga, cleaning, baking, statistics of different subjects and many more. Quite often, transitioning from the subject of interest will be quite difficult.

The fourth group of behaviours, covered under their respective headings, relates to SENSORY SENSITIVITIES, which includes PAIN.

Synaesthesia – see Sensory sensitivities

T

Technology (assistive and entertainment)

Technology has made differences to the lives of people with ASD. While there is much hype about the benefits of assistive technologies, it is important that your child is paired with ability and developmentally appropriate devices/games. Earlier manual and relatively inexpensive tools, sometimes now called 'dumb'ware, such as the incredibly helpful Makaton (named for its inventors), PECS (Picture Exchange Communication System) and even Auslan (Australian), BSL (British) and ASL (American) sign languages, are still most effective and many parents and their children return to them, often only after having spent time and money on trying modern technology. Most new computer-based assistive technologies await scientific validation. The most helpful appear to be variations (sometimes clumsy) on manual systems mentioned above, used for many decades.

All technology used should improve your child's experience. Be wary of facilitated communication devices that purport, usually with an operator's assistance, to help your child communicate. Most of these have not stood up to independent review.

Parents do report that some children become increasingly motivated, show better concentration, and develop a sense of agency and mastery. It may even help your child engage in learning different ways of understanding and coping with their emotions and adapting to social situations. Technology is but one of a range of tools you can use to help your child.

Technology as entertainment, with a particular caution about highly self-stimulatory games, should always be used discerningly, in a limited way and as far as possible removed from TOKEN REWARD SYSTEMS. If previously used in the early stages of transitioning to a token system, console or computer games may need to be incorporated. There is increasing research to indicate that games may be addictive and that the production of the neurotransmitter dopamine is implicated. Observing children while they are playing certain games, and their heightened aggression following playing, should cause pause for consideration of their use.

Theory of Mind

Theory of Mind appears to be an innate potential in the majority of typical people. Being able to attribute mental states to others and understanding them as causes of behaviour is a significant protective factor in social interactions and its absence a social disability. People diagnosed with autism have considerable difficulty determining the mental states of others and lack of awareness of their own mental states. These are called Theory of Mind abilities. It is the ability to understand or form a theory of what their own and others' thoughts, beliefs, values and desires are and how they may influence their lives. Their lack of attention to others' facial expressions (see FACIAL BLINDNESS) may explain why people with autism show deficits in Theory of Mind.

One view of Theory of Mind suggests that it plays a role in attributing (attribution theory) mental states, such as different emotions, to others as well as imaginative PLAY. Developmental psychology research suggests that a child's (and adult's) ability to imitate others (as in social learning theory[87]) is the basis of both a Theory of Mind and other social-cognitive achievements such as perspective-taking and empathy. Given that children with ASD may not have the 'hardware' or 'programming' to pay attention to other people's faces, this may partly explain the difficulty in modelling behaviour and therefore the deficits in social learning.

The difficulty with facial recognition and whether *any* children younger than three or four years old can have a Theory of Mind is a topic of debate among researchers. Certainly, most parents would attest to feeling a response to their own emotional states from a young infant. Whether this involves the infant's thoughts or is only a behavioural mirroring is conjecture. The latter, too, will involve the infant visually attending to expression from their parent. In ASD the absence of this 'instinct', often noticed to their distress by parents of infants who don't like to be held, cuddled, fed and who exhibit intense distress for no discernible reason, may be the root of many social problems (see EMPATHY). Simon Baron-Cohen[88] identified that an infant's understanding of attention in others is a 'critical precursor' to the development of Theory of Mind. That one person shares an object of interest by pointing and the other person assesses the object as either of interest or not, indicating so to the first, may be the early development of learning and even the forming of identity. Why does one person prefer chocolate and another strawberry ice cream? Seeing can initiate beliefs about the world; safe or unsafe and desired or rejected (for example ice cream). Without having some notion of other people's minds, and that they have their own thoughts, can result in not understanding that attention needs to be attracted, directed and shared in order to have a joint experience when the child notices an object or finds it of interest. Without this appreciation, becoming self-focused seems inevitable.

Appreciating attention, understanding of others' thoughts, beliefs, desires and intentions, combined with imitative experience (social learning) with other people, are keys to the theory of others' minds and sharing experiences.

Therapies

ASD is said to be a 'fad magnet'. There are many suggested treatments for ASD and its different components. The gold standard for medical research is a Cochrane Review[89] or summary of all discoverable research on a topic. There are few treatments to assist with ASD that have even the slightest scientific validation. EARLY INTERVENTION, or Early Intensive Behavioural Intervention, including APPLIED BEHAVIOUR ANALYSIS or Functional Behavioural Analysis and other related techniques are the only therapies that earn the accolade that Cochrane Reviews offer only after rigorous analysis: 'There is some evidence that EIBI is an effective behavioural treatment for some children with ASD.' There is also some benefit attributed to

Music Therapy, although this seems to be when offered in conjunction with EIBI.

While many offered therapies may afford some entertainment value to the child and may be beneficial from that perspective, their costs and benefits need to be evaluated in the context of what can make a difference and the time and money used unnecessarily.

While almost all people working in the area of ASD are well intentioned, there are unfortunately charlatans everywhere. Most want, for your child, what you as their parent wants. ASD is a condition where progress can be slow and needs a concerted effort. Frustration may result in parents and professionals, with an understandable attraction to seemingly instant and miraculous 'cures'. For example, while some medications may be helpful for some children with particular problems, in this case depression, a Cochrane Review of SSRIs (current generation anti-depressant medication called selective serotonin reuptake inhibitors) for treating autism found that '[t]here is no evidence of effect of SSRIs in children (with ASD) and emerging evidence of harm.' You and your trusted ASD professional are in the best position to make decisions about treatment. Be aware that accrediting bodies of some professions may endorse approaches that have even been found to be harmful. One of considerable concern is the practice of physical spinal manipulation interventions on infants with autism. The greatest care is urged.

Tics

Tics are defined by one or many brief repeated movements or sounds that are involuntary. Tic disorders are specific and differ from STEREOTYPIES, habits or compulsions. While people of all abilities, intelligence and ages can develop tic disorders, they are most common in children, and more likely to occur in boys than girls. It is now generally accepted that tics are related to ANXIETY, in the absence of other neurological reasons such as seizures and brain injury, meaning that they may be amenable to being managed or reduced by dealing with the anxiety, depression or other conditions that may be causing them.

There appear to be differences between tics in children with and without ASD. Children with ASD seem to have little awareness of their tics even when pointed out to them, whereas typical children may try to suppress their tics as a result of how they may appear to others, increasing their anxiety in the process and exacerbating the tics as a result. This may be one of the areas where being on the spectrum could be an advantage.

The prevalence of simple tics in school-age children, with the more common tics of eye twitching and blinking, coughing, throat clearing, sniffing and facial twitching, is much higher than the usually quite complex tics in the much publicised Tourette's Syndrome. Tourette's is an inherited neurological and possibly developmental disorder with typical onset in childhood. It is characterised by multiple physical tics and for formal diagnosis at least one vocal tic, which may be more discernible as a repeated noise. The tics may come and go, may be suppressed temporarily and are usually, in typical people, preceded by the person knowing they are about to happen. Tourette's is probably more common in ASD than in the general population (3.8 per cent of children and adolescents aged 5 to 18)[90] and usually improves as people age, although some may have tics throughout their lives. Most people associate Tourette's with vocalising obscene words or socially inappropriate and derogatory remarks (coprolalia), but this specific symptom is present in only a very few people with symptoms. This is also true of those people who have ASD.

Tics may be exhibited as quite complex routines. One young teenager, when anxious, would pace in a circle leaning inwards with one hand on his hip and the other waving in the air. At various times he would reach out and deliberately and firmly touch, slap or flick chairs, tables, desks, lamps and the walls. All the while he would speak in a pressured and uninterruptible monologue about a special interest while sniffing and sighing deeply. Even when asked directly as to what he was doing, he would typically only briefly respond with 'Nothing! Why?' and perhaps some semblance of surprise. When pointed out that he was walking in circles flicking and tapping, he would respond 'No, I'm not', while continuing.

Children with ASD may become perseverative about certain words or even echolalic and this may give an appearance of Tourette's, but in such cases the expression is usually reinforced behaviour caused by some other trigger. Swearing learned at school by children with cognitive impairment may be reinforced by classmates laughing. This would need to be addressed at school before the swearing can be extinguished. Most cases of tics are mild and the severity of tics decreases for most children as they pass through adolescence. Tourette's does not adversely affect intelligence or life expectancy. Certain medications and therapies can help when their use is warranted. Psychoeducation is an important part of any treatment, and explanations and reassurance alone can be effective in adolescents, although much less so than in children. Children with ASD may be quite unaware of their tics and may be bullied for having them (see BULLYING).

Toileting

Toilet training should be behavioural and is not necessarily delayed or more complex with children with ASD unless there is a comorbid physical disability. Remember, children in developing countries usually learn to first indicate their need to toilet before their first year and subsequently go by themselves in their second year, although cleaning and dressing take longer. Disposable nappies are not usually available or affordable. While there are all sorts of warnings about early toileting on the internet, again, children in developing countries seem to have few of the psychological issues with toileting that frequently afflict those in some Western countries.

The earliest possible time should be chosen for toilet training, but sensible and natural preparation may be necessary. Toileting is the most normal of behaviours, and in the absence of physical disabilities should be well within the grasp of most children, although cleaning afterwards may be more challenging, given it is not obvious. It is suggested that, as far as possible, intermediate steps be avoided given that children with ASD are largely unable to generalise. While there are obviously practical difficulties for a child with ASD, learning to toilet on a potty may require entirely new teaching to progress to a toilet. Avoid fancy potties that are engaging and distracting as they may be difficult to transition as your child grows. One reason toileting can take longer is because of the communication challenges associated with children with ASD and our modern approach to toileting in contemporary homes.

As with other desired behaviours you may want your child to develop, toilet training is enabled by modelling, visual aids, encouragement and rewards, support and SOCIAL STORIES™. Remember that your child's progress with toilet training may be affected by sensory overload and you may have minor setbacks along the way.

Treat the toilet training as an entire process from eating (and drinking) through feeling a full stomach to going to the toilet. Anyone can demonstrate this to a toddler by sticking out their own stomach, obviously patting it and making a big show of going to the toilet. Attach the words you use in your family to each action, for example, 'big dinner', 'full stomach'; demonstrate 'go to toilet', 'do a poo', 'clean up', flush, 'bye bye poo', wave, 'all good', and 'wash hands'.

Try to put yourself in your child's place. Imagine you are a child with ASD who already has difficulty in understanding all the different things that happen to you and around you. It is all personal. In regard to toileting, you watch people in your family and others disappear into the same room, which possibly you have never entered. You hear strange (loud?) noises for a while. After some time people come out, possibly with a red face, maybe dressing as they walk, then washing their hands; something else you don't understand. You have grown up with a nappy or diaper, so have never seen your faeces or what happens to them. You are now as a child put on a potty or toilet, and you see part of your body coming out. It may be interesting, and you may wish to play with it. You may even try to explore from where it came. If a little older, you may think you have lost part of your body and become distressed.

The following may be uncomfortable for some parents. Encourage immediate family, when at home alone, to explain going to the toilet, as in 'I'm going to the toilet' or as described earlier, following a meal. Everyone should use simple and the same language. For a young child trying to understand their world, bathroom, toilet, 'poo', 'doodoos' or 'number two' are just confusing. Pick one word for the family to use and stay with it. Remember, your child with ASD may be using the same word 20 years later. For the easiest approach, have adults and other older children go to the toilet with the door open. Allow the child to come in with you and even sit in the bathroom with you, once old enough to do so, maybe on a small chair if their motor skills and room permit (yes, I can imagine what you are thinking).

Anticipate your child's toileting needs, preferably to a timetable. Typically, babies toilet shortly after feeding. From as early as possible, learn to recognise your child's 'pre-wee' and 'pre-poo' signs; their little face changes, signs of concentration, burps and wind. Take them to the potty, basin or toilet and, while holding their legs, hold their bottoms over the receptacle. Wait until they produce. Using command toileting by taking them to a toilet and allowing them to go naturally, while holding them and repeating, usually works; if not, gently lifting their knees to their chest will usually do the job – this is practised in many developing countries. If they don't need to go, schedule it an hour later. Use encouraging but simple phrases and a quiet and calm approach. 'Toilet time!', 'Next time!', 'Well done!', for example.

Anecdotally, there is substantial difference in toileting practice between developed and developing countries, with parents in the latter expecting continence and working towards self-toileting much earlier than parents in Western countries. In developing countries the limited availability of nappies (diapers), washing powder and disinfectants makes such earlier continence an important milestone. It may appear politically incorrect or be impolite to make the comparison but even animals are easily trained to toilet, and yet we expect our children to do so spontaneously or wait until they are much older and we become concerned. (See Parenting Science website for useful information.[91])

There are many most peculiar statements on the internet about how late children may be 'emotionally' ready to self-toilet. They often indicate between 18 and 48 months. Please be cautious of any site sponsored by a company that may make profit from delayed toileting. In developing countries, from a few days after birth children are often regularly, and after meals, command toileted. With children this can be a confidence-instilling developmental event. Regular recognition of their achievement when they are infants and toddlers is important. So too is avoiding making a big deal about accidents.

While having fun around changing can be a bonding time for parent and child, it is also a reinforcement of unwanted behaviour. Try to approach it in an objective and almost efficient manner. Use the time you save to cuddle, feed and play enjoyably and meaningfully with your child when those activities are the focus of your intentions, separately from changing. This also, and perhaps more so, creates significant and enjoyable bonding.

It is quite possible to have some children with ASD with no language go to the toilet by themselves, but not clean and dress, by one year of age. If it takes longer, stay calm. If first self-toileting has not occurred by 18 months, obtain advice from a medical practitioner, expert occupational therapist or ASD-familiar clinical psychologist. Be aware, though, that first self-toileting may not occur until even 30 months. However, do persevere as this will make all your lives so much easier and better! (See also DEFECATING, URINATING and FAECAL SMEARING.)

Token reward systems

Often referred to as a 'token economy', this refers to a system of providing positive reinforcement by giving tokens for behaving in specific (desired) ways or for completing tasks as desired. Tokens are used to increase the frequency of a behaviour or to strengthen the likelihood of children enacting a specific behaviour. Depending on development, children are able to accumulate or exchange their tokens for items or activities that they find desirable or attractive. Token economies can be used for any target (desired) behaviour, from using the toilet to saying hello or goodbye to their siblings. When using a token economy, it is important that you have a 'map', or a visual schedule, in a highly visible place in the house (or school) which simply states what the child needs to do and is working to. A list of desired appropriate behaviours, stated in positive and specific terms, should also be prominent. For example, if room tidying is on the list, one way to describe it is 'Place all items in your room in their proper place.' Obviously, to do this the child will first need to know what is meant by the proper place. Labelling drawers and shelves or indicating by pictures is the most helpful approach.

For the token system, the simplest strategy may be to break the day into different periods depending on age, such as before school, school, after school and evening. Three stickers or tokens or green ticks on a chart are available for each period. Three awarded for excellence, two for a minor error or none (one alone is never awarded, as research shows that children do not differentiate as much between zero and one, or between one and two, but see a significant distinction between zero and two). The tokens may be traded towards 15 minutes of technology, a Pokémon card, a certificate or some other *nominal* reward, or they can be accumulated so that when a significant number are earned there may be a visit to a pre-determined film or theme park. These treats should then not be available without the tokens having been earned. Tokens should never be used for food, money or high-value items. Money and food should not be used as rewards.

Future highly desirable events may be age-appropriate longer term goals and are most helpful for behaviour change. Working towards learning to drive by accumulating driving lessons has kept one teenager on track for 12 months.

Caution: Always have the entire system designed and agreed by all adults before implementing. Schools and teachers will need to be part of the strategy.

Transitions

Transitioning between tasks is something we all do many times every day. For children with ASD this can be particularly challenging. Recent research suggests this may be linked to cortisol production. It has nothing to do with the child being naughty. Careful preparation and planning is vital through periods of transition (when they are likely to be much more challenging). You can help prepare your child for all transitions by employing the following strategies:

- From toddler age use a pictorial visual schedule even if they can't read; it's good training for you and good learning for them. Pictures of a sunrise for morning, full sun for day, stars for night, and so on.

- Use a visual timer so children can see how long they have before they have to switch tasks (e.g. Time Timers[92]).

- Continually tell your child what is happening on the basis of No Surprises.

- Use objects, photos or words (e.g. a photo of people they will see or of the building they will be going to next).

- Use simple written, verbal and visual sequential instruction, using a *'first, then'* approach. For example: '*First* you have free play on the carpet until 12.20, and *then* you move to the playground for lunch until 1pm.' For younger children use clock face visuals to show them times and help them learn about time. Then a picture of a playground and then a sandwich, for example.

- Having numbered boxes with tasks (toys) with which to progressively interact through the day, including boxes with food pictures for meals, will help them establish patterns and avoid anxiety.

- Boxes can also be used to show when Mummy or Daddy return from work, siblings from school, when baths are, and so on.

- Having a box with the word 'finished' clearly labelled on the side (i.e. 'the finished box'), where all completed work is placed throughout the day, can also help children transition between tasks.

- Use transitioning SOCIAL STORIES™.

As with other routine strategies, try to be consistent in your application of the strategies. They help people with ASD learn independence and move more easily between activities and locations.

Transitioning from one school to another or from school to work are major issues in the lives of children with ASD. These are unlikely to progress without significant support, including perhaps from professionals. Planning should begin at least a year in advance and the strategy at least six months before the change occurs. A detailed, pictorial workbook is the best transition tracking strategy for use by everyone, including the child.

U

Understanding

Understanding is two-way. Often children with autism cannot understand what other people are thinking, feeling or doing, and they may also have trouble communicating. They may also not understand information, and particularly so at school. They may have a ceiling to their understanding of information that is provided in a particular way (perhaps visually or verbally or a particular rate of information provision). They may be great at the elements of English such as spelling, grammar and reading but may have difficulty in writing even simple essays. They may not understand that they need to correct drafts.

Similarly, people who are *not* on the spectrum may have trouble understanding the behaviour of people with ASD. People with ASD also may have no understanding of other people with ASD. To other people, this behaviour can appear perplexing and sometimes even distressing. This is because people who are on the autism spectrum usually enjoy limited, repetitive or restrictive behaviours and sometimes have MELTDOWNS. This, combined with difficulties in social interactions, including verbal and non-verbal communication, means typical people often simply do not understand what is happening or why someone with ASD will say (or not say) certain things or act the way they do. There is a steep learning curve associated with being the parent of a child on the spectrum despite the fact that learning is life-long. One of the greatest gifts you can give your child and yourself is to be loving, compassionate and understanding of the fact that you are all going through a process, which is not always going to be easy. Sometimes the best thing can be to pause for a few seconds and simply acknowledge that you are *all* going through a tough moment. (See also CELEBRATION.)

Unusual (see also Idiosyncrasies and Quirky)

You may sometimes think that your child's responses are unusual, or you may have received feedback from others that they seem unusual. While this can be communicated in ways that further add to the stigma and confusion around having ASD, *all* children sometimes exhibit unusual responses or behaviour. What will become apparent over time is that you notice your child's normal responses and behaviours. These may occur at unusual times; or for an unusually extended period, perhaps, the absence of a particular behaviour is unusual to you. Once you become familiar with these 'unusual' behaviours, you will adapt to them and be able to take them on board as being another one of your child's unique attributes. Where necessary they may warrant changing.

Urinating (involuntary urination, urinary incontinence, enuresis) (see also Toileting and Defecating)

The terms involuntary urination, urinary incontinence and enuresis (nocturnal and diurnal) may be used interchangeably and imply similar behaviour. They all refer to wetting after the age when it is usually expected to be controlled. Anecdotally it seems more present in developed countries and seems to have a number of possible individual causes which are poorly understood, any of which may be combined in children with the problem. It is not limited to children with ASD, being as common in typical children. It may come and go to make it even more difficult to treat. After the age of five, night-time wetting is more common than daytime wetting in boys and typically it is more common in boys than girls. Primary consideration is, as far as possible, to reduce anxiety around the wetting. Parents (and other significant adults) who can remain calm are most likely to be helpful in reducing the number of accidents and eliminating enuresis. Approach accidents with practical remedies, maybe just helping them clean at the time, avoid any escalation of stress for the child who will already be feeling embarrassed, and be supportive.

While concerned parents are inclined to attempt all types of remedies including alarms, heavy blankets, removal of blankets and fans, hypnosis, therapies, music and complementary medicine, these may only serve to increase anxiety and make the problem worse. While some of these may work for some children, in practice there is little evidence for most.

Medication

There are two quite different types of prescription medications typically used to try to help with enuresis. They are Tofranil (imipramine) and Minirin (desmopressin). If your doctor first tries one and it doesn't work, the other may be effective. Your doctor may insist that you try a nocturnal enuresis alarm before they prescribe the medication. It is important to ensure that they understand that your child has ASD and may be prone to high anxiety. This is significant due to the recent discovery of the differences in cortisol production in children with ASD.

Nocturnal (night-time – usually asleep) and diurnal (daytime) enuresis

From the age of five, wetting at night becomes more common than daytime involuntary wetting in boys. The cause is largely unknown but several strategies have been shown to help. Children who wet while asleep are mostly mentally, physically and emotionally typical. There appears to be a hereditary element. Experts believe that undetermined genes are involved. Factors identified, including in children with ASD, quite commonly are unidentified urinary tract infections, and in all children are anxiety, possible delayed actual physical development, urine overproduction, bladder size, and deeper deep-sleep phases and therefore a related inability, while asleep, to realise that their bladder is full.

Anxiety

Anxiety-causing events in the lives of children of two to four years may lead to incontinence, either before they achieve complete bladder control or even after they have done so. Well after four years, anxiety may lead to wetting even into the teens and after the child has been dry for some time. Any anxiety-provoking event, including mental trauma, domestic violence, abuse, unfamiliar social situations, moving home, changing school or the unexpected such as the birth of a sibling, may cause wetting. The incontinence also causes anxiety and adult responses of dealing with it in a low-key manner are important to minimise the anxiety. Daytime wetting can cause embarrassment and anxiety that may also lead to wetting at night.

Delayed physical development

Between the ages of five and ten, incontinence may be the result of anxiety, a small bladder, deep or long sleep and underdevelopment of the body's signals to the brain. This tends to self-correct as the child grows and natural responses progressively develop.

Excessive output of urine during sleep

The antidiuretic hormone normally slows urine production, and the body produces more antidiuretic hormone during sleep. If their body does not produce enough antidiuretic hormone at night, the child's bladder can become too full. If a child is a deep sleeper or otherwise does not respond and wake to urinate, then wetting may occur.

Genetics

In 1995, researchers in Denmark announced that they had found a site on human chromosome 13 that may be implicated in night-time wetting. Research indicates that if *both* parents were delayed in becoming continent, then 77 per cent of their children will be; and if only *one* parent was delayed, then 44 per cent of their offspring will be. Much more research is needed, though.

Obstructive sleep apnoea (OSA)

While OSA, or breathing interruption, is much more common in adults, people who may be overweight and those adults who have respiratory conditions, it is also common in children, often a result of inflamed or enlarged tonsils or adenoids. Other indications, even in young children, of OSA may include any of snoring, mouth breathing, ear, nose and throat infections, choking and over-tiredness and drowsiness during daytime activities. Successful treatment of OSA may also resolve the night-time incontinence if it is linked.

Structural problems

In limited cases incontinence is caused by physical issues in the urinary (or renal) system. Urinary reflux is where urine backs up into one or both urinary ducts (ureters). As a result it can cause urinary tract infections and incontinence. Most seldom a blocked bladder or urethra may cause incontinence. There are physical disabilities associated with nerve damage that can also cause incontinence, although this will be recognised through other symptoms.

Diurnal enuresis

Daytime incontinence that is not associated with urinary infection or physical disabilities is less common than night-time incontinence and tends to spontaneously stop much earlier. In ASD, daytime incontinence may be related to distraction of special interests or other activities, obsessions that may prevent the child from using strange toilets, for example, at school, unwilling to draw attention to themselves in class by indicating they may need to use a toilet or just being unaware that the full bladder sensation should receive attention. Children with daytime incontinence may have unusual voiding habits, the most common being infrequent voiding or deliberate retention for any number of reasons. This incontinence occurs more often in girls than in boys and appears to be often related to anxiety.

As a general rule, always eliminate obvious physical conditions such as infection before seeking more complex causes and solutions.

V

Victory – see Celebration

W

Writing

For most children (and adults) with ASD, writing can be a major challenge and cause of great distress. All manner of aids and assistive devices, pencils with triangular grips, admonishment and punishment, often out of teacher frustration, make little or no difference to the writing but may seriously and detrimentally impact self-esteem (see IDENTITY). Wrist-strengthening is another unhelpful traditional remedy. In the 21st century we should really ask why this technology, as outdated as an abacus, is so important as to be worth causing distress in our children. All the evidence is for a difference in their brain, rather than in their fingers, hand or wrist. There is no evidence for duct-taping of pencils to hands in certain positions, taping hands behind backs and boring wrist-strengthening exercises with rubber bands and yet these are still currently pursued. We are as yet unable to devise specific brain exercises to remedy this difficulty and would do best to provide assistive strategies instead of those that children see as punitive.

For actual writing tasks there may also be complications. These may be caused by problems with EXECUTIVE

FUNCTION and ANXIETY. Further points of reference are PERFECTIONISM and PROCRASTINATION.

Establishing a comprehensive understanding of how a writing task should be done from very early on will save inordinate difficulty later. Children with ASD, unless directly taught, do not have an idea that they may themselves harbour different and sometimes contradictory views of the same subject. They will typically invest in the first thought, correct or incorrect, and *may* but won't always expand on that, refusing any direction to examine it from a different perspective. This is an element of black/white or dichotomous thinking described in executive function. From the earliest of their learning they will need to know to check their work and look for errors, and in so doing also learn to correct drafts of essays later in their schooling. The earlier that the ideas are introduced, the more likely they are to be effectively learned.

X

Fragile-X Syndrome (FXS)

FXS causes a range of functioning across domains, similarly to ASD. It is, however, in contradistinction, a specific, identifiable condition with a known genetic cause. ASD is instead identified by a cluster of symptoms rather than a specific condition. ASD is believed to have many causes, although unravelling them has so far, for the most part, not been successful. It has long been recognised, by parents, educators and clinicians, that there is overlap between FXS and ASD in that some people with FXS exhibit signs and symptoms of ASD and some do not. Only recently has the possibility been raised that the two conditions may have considerably more overlap than previously thought. Researchers are investigating whether this overlap may extend beyond the often-identified behavioural similarities to perhaps include genetic or biological markers as well. Although FXS accounts for only a small proportion of ASD, research shows that it is the leading known single-gene cause of ASD. That research may prove to have far-reaching effects.

Y

Why not?

I hear you say 'Why?' Always 'Why?' You see things; and you say 'Why?' But I dream things that never were; and I say 'Why not?'

George Bernard Shaw (1856–1950)

The worst thing you can do is nothing [on teaching children with autism].

Temple Grandin

In an ideal world the scientist should find a method to prevent the most severe forms of autism but allow the milder forms to survive. After all, the really social people did not invent the first stone spear. It was probably invented by an Aspie who chipped away at rocks while the other people socialized around the campfire. Without autism traits we might still be living in caves.

Temple Grandin[93]

Z

Zyzzyva

For no other reason than that it is the last letter in the alphabet and 'zyzzyva' the last word in an English dictionary. Such interesting snippets of information are frequently provided by people with ASD and children remain the more spontaneous and delightful, not having their own special excitement (which they may never explicitly exhibit) diminished by a world limited in its understanding and acceptance of them. In your time with a little person with ASD and as they develop and as they often need more support for longer than typical children, you will be delighted and frustrated, irritated and distressed, only in the pits of despair to be raised up by one of their attractive quirks.

Allow yourself the support and occasional distancing to be also able to realise the pleasure of their developing. They will typically shrug it off as they are quite disinclined to recognise anything as remarkable, except for their special interest and they won't think to engage others in it.

The most frustrating, ever, long-term client was autistic. He never spoke and exhibited every challenging behaviour imaginable and some quite unimaginable. He had a tragic background and for many consultations attended with his two burly male escorts as was required by his care team, notwithstanding his small size. This time he again entered the consulting room as usual without making eye contact. He thrust his hand into his pocket and pulled out a chocolate bar, saying only his first public word ever, 'Here!'

It was as well he never looked at me, as tears rolled down my face, and he wouldn't have been able to understand. He used that week's pocket money to buy the chocolate from a vending machine in the home where he stayed. He saw me for three more years, by when he had acquired some words and was quite adept at PECS (Picture Exchange Communication System). His behaviour improved, and he was working two hours per day at a nursery with a caring owner.

We must always support our children's weaknesses and challenge their strengths, but above all, there is always room for improvement in their lives. The last word isn't zyzzyva, it's NEVER GIVE UP!

Notes

1. American Psychiatric Association (2013) *Diagnostic and Statistical Manual of Mental Disorders (5th Edition).* Arlington, VA: American Psychiatry Publishing.

2. American Psychiatric Association (2000) *Diagnostic and Statistical Manual of Mental Disorders (4th Edition).* Arlington, VA: American Psychiatry Publishing.

3. Zimmer, M., and Desch, L. (2012) 'Sensory integration therapies for children with developmental and behavioural disorders.' *Official Journal of the American Academy of Paediatrics.* doi: 10.1542/peds.2012-0876.

4. McPartland, J.C., Reichow, B., and Volkmar, F.R. (2012) 'Sensitivity and specificity of proposed *DSM-5* diagnostic criteria for Autism Spectrum Disorder.' *Journal of the American Academy of Child & Adolescent Psychiatry 51,* 4, 368–383. doi: http://dx.doi.org/10.1016/j.jaac.2012.01.007.

5. Stephen Wiltshire (2016) *Stephen Wiltshire: Biography.* Available at www.stephenwiltshire.co.uk/biography.aspx, accessed on 25 July 2016.

6. Howling, P., and Asgharian, A. (1999) 'The diagnosis of autism and Asperger's Syndrome: Findings from a survey of 770 families.' *Developmental Medicine & Child Neurology 41,* 12, 834–839. doi: 10.1111/j.1469-8749.1999.tb00550.x.

7. Chawarska, K., Paul, R., Klin, A., Hannigen, S., Dichtel, L.E., and Volmar, F. (2007) 'Parental recognition of development problems in toddlers with Autism Spectrum Disorder.' *Journal of Autism and Developmental Disorders 37,* 1, 62–67. doi: 10.1007/s10803-006-0330-8.

8. Gliga, T., Bedford, R., Charman, T., and Johnson, M. (2015) 'Enhanced visual search in infancy predicts emerging autism symptoms.' *Current Biology 25,* 1727–1730. doi: http://dx.doi.org/10.1016/j.cub.2015.05.011.

9. Grandin, T., and Panek, R. (2013) *The Autistic Brain: Thinking Across the Spectrum.* New York, NY: Houghton Mifflin Harcourt.

10. O'Haire, M.E., McKenzie, S.J., Beck, A.M., and Slaughter, V. (2015) 'Animals may act as social buffers: Skin conductance arousal in children with autism spectrum disorder in a social context.' *Developmental Psychobiology 57*, 5, 584–595. doi: 10.1002/dev.21310.

11. Grandgeorge, M., Torjman, S., Lazartigues, A., Lemonnier, E., Deleau, M., and Hausberger, M. (2012) 'Does pet arrival trigger prosocial behaviours in individuals with autism?' *PLoS One 7*, 8. doi: 10.1371/journal.pone.0041739.

12. Guide Dogs Australia (n.d.) *Autism Assistance Dogs.* Available at www.guidedogs.org.au/autism-assistance-dogs, accessed on 25 July 2016.

13. Brosnan, M., Turner-Cobb, J., Munro-Naan, Z., and Jessop, D. (2009) 'Absence of a normal cortisol awakening response (CAR) in adolescent males with Asperger Syndrome (ASD).' *Psychoneuroendocrinology 34*, 7, 1095–1100. doi: 10.1016/j.psyneuen.2009.02.011.

14. Putnam, S.K., Lopata, C., Thomeer, M.L., Volker, M.A., and Rodgers, J.D. (2015) 'Salivary cortisol levels and diurnal patterns in children with Autism Spectrum Disorder.' *Journal of Developmental and Physical Disabilities 27*, 4, 453–465. doi: 10.1007/s10882-015-9428-2.

15. Lovaas, O.I. (1987) 'Behavioural treatment and normal educational and intellectual functioning in young autistic children.' *Journal of Consulting and Clinical Psychology 55*, 1 , 3–9. doi: 10.1037/0022-006X.55.1.3.

16. *Cochrane Database of Systematic Reviews (CDSR)* Available at www.cochranelibrary.com/cochrane-database-of-systematic-reviews, accessed on 25 July 2016.

17. O'Reily, B., and Wicks, K. (2016) *The Complete Autism Handbook (3rd Edition).* Edgecliffe, NSW: Ventura Press.

18. Davis, N.O., and Kollins, S.H. (2012) 'Treatment for co-occurring Attention Deficit/Hyperactivity Disorder and Autism Spectrum Disorder.' *Neurotherapeutics 9*, 3, 518–530. doi: 10.1007/s13311-012-0126-9.

19. Miodovnik, A., Harstad, E., Sideridis, G., and Huntington, N. (2015) 'Timing and the diagnosis of Attention-Deficit/Hyperactivity Disorder and Autism Spectrum Disorder.' *Paediatric 136*, 4, 830–837. doi: 10.1542/peds.2015-1502.

20. Crawford, M.W., Vernon, A.B., and Harden, K. (2015) 'Self regulation of breathing as a primary treatment for anxiety.' *Applied Psychophysiology and Biofeedback 40*, 2, 107–115. doi: 10.1007/s10484-015-9279-8.

21. Bonafide, C.P., Brady, P.W., Keren, R., Conway, P.H., Marsolo, K., and Daymont, C. (2013) 'Development of heart and respiratory rate percentile curve for hospitalized children.' *Paediatrics 131*, 4, 1150–1157. doi: 10.1542/peds.2012-2443.

22. Dwyer, R. (2011) *Normal Horse Temperature, Breathing Rate, Heart Rate.* Available at www.thehorse.com/articles/27822/normal-horse-temperature-heart-rate-breathing-rate, accessed on 25 July 2016.

23. Gray, C. (2002) *My Social Stories.* London and Philadelphia: Jessica Kingsley Publishers.

24. Gray, C. (1994) *Comic Strip Conversations.* Arlington, TX: Jenison Public Schools.

25. Hill, E.L. (2004) 'Evaluating the theory of executive dysfunction in autism.' *Developmental Review 24,* 2, 189–233. doi:10.1016/j.dr.2004.01.001.

26. Anderson, V., Levin, H.S., and Jacobs, R. (2002) 'Executive Functions after Frontal Lobe Injury: A Developmental Perspective.' In D.T. Stuss and R.T. Knight (eds) *Principles of Frontal Lobe Function.* Oxford: Oxford University Press. doi: 10.1093/acprof:oso/9780195134971.003.0030.

27. Oono, I.P., Honey, E.J., and McConachie, H. (2013) 'Parent-mediated early intervention for young children with autism spectrum disorders.' *Cochrane Database of Systematic Reviews 4.* doi: 10.1002/14651858.CD009774.pub2.

28. Roberts, J.M.A., and Prior, M. (2006) *A Review of the Research to Identify the Most Effective Models of Practice in Early Intervention of Children with Autism Spectrum Disorders.* Australia: Australian Government Department of Health and Ageing.

29. Filipek, P.A., Accardo, P.J., Baranek, G.T., Cook, E.H., *et al.* (1999) 'The screening and diagnosis of Autistic Spectrum Disorder.' *Journal of Autism Developmental Disorders 29,* 6, 439–484. doi: 10.1023/A:1021943802493.

30. Filipek, P.A., Accardo, P.J., Baranek, G.T., Cook, E.H., *et al.* (1999) 'The screening and diagnosis of Autistic Spectrum Disorder.' *Journal of Autism Developmental Disorders 29,* 6, 439–484. doi: 10.1023/A:1021943802493.

31. Filipek, P.A., Accardo, P.J., Baranek, G.T., Cook, E.H., *et al.* (1999) 'The screening and diagnosis of Autistic Spectrum Disorder.' *Journal of Autism Developmental Disorders 29,* 6, 439–484. doi: 10.1023/A:1021943802493.

32. Smith, T. (2001) 'Discrete trial training in the treatment of autism.' *Focus on Autism and Other Developmental Disabilities 16,* 86–92. doi: 10.1177/108835760101600204.

33. Skinner, B.F. (1957) *Verbal Behaviour.* New York, NY: Copley.

34. Johnston, T., and Schembri, A. (2007) *Australian Sign Language (Auslan): An Introduction to Sign Language Linguistics.* Cambridge: Cambridge University Press.

35. Yoon, S.Y., and Bennett, G.M. (2000) 'Effects of a stimulus-stimulus pairing procedure on conditioning vocal sounds as reinforcers.' *Analysis of Verbal Behaviour 17*, 75–88.

36. Golarai, G., Grill-Spector, K., and Reis, A.L. (2006) 'Autism and the development of face processing.' *Clinical Neuroscience Research 6*, 145–160. doi:10.1016/j.cnr.2006.08.001.

37. Hothersall, D. (2003) *History of Psychology (4th Edition)*. New York, NY: McGraw-Hill.

38. Tucker, M. (2010) *Gestalt Principles Applied in Design*. Available at www.sixrevisions.com/web_design/gestalt-principles-applied-in-design, accessed on 25 July 2016.

39. von der Heydt, R., Peterhans, E., and Baumgartner, G. (1984) 'Illusory contours and cortical neuron responses.' *Science 224*, 4654, 1260–1262. doi: 10.1126/science.6539501.

40. Iwatani, T. (1980) *Pac-Man*. Namco, Japan: Namco.

41. O'Brien, J., Spencer, J., Girges, C., Johnston, A., and Hill, H. (2014) 'Impaired perception of facial motion in autism spectrum disorder.' *PLoS One 9*, 7, 1–6. doi: 10.1371/journal.pone.0102173.

42. Duchaine, B., Murray, H., Turner, M., White, S., and Garrido, L. (2009) 'Normal social cognition in developmental prosopagnosia.' *Cognitive Neuropsychology 26*, 7, 620–634. doi: 10.1080/02643291003616145.

43. Gray, C. (1994) *Comic Strip Conversations*. Available at www.autism.org.uk/about/strategies/social-stories-comic-strips/comic-strip-conversations.aspx, accessed on 25 July 2016.

44. GBD 2013 Mortality and Causes of Death Collaborators (2015) 'Global, regional and national age-sex specific all-cause and cause-specific mortality for 240 causes of death, 1990–2013: A systematic analysis for the Global Burden of Disease Study 2013.' *Lancet 385*, 9963, 117–171. doi: 10.1016/S0140-6736(14)61682-2.

45. Theroux, L. (2012, 19 April) *Extreme Love: Autism*. United Kingdom: BBC UK.

46. Simone, R. (2010) *Aspergirls: Empowering Females with Asperger's Syndrome*. London: Jessica Kingsley Publishers.

47. American Psychiatric Association (2000) *Diagnostic and Statistical Manual of Mental Disorders (4th Edition, text rev.)*. Washington, DC: American Psychiatry Publishing.

48. Kerr, P.L., Meuhlenkamp, J.J., and Turner, J.M. (2010) 'Non-suicidal self-injury: A review of current research for family medicine and primary care physicians.' *Journal of American Board of Family Medicine 3*, 240–259. doi:10.3122/jabfm.2010.02.090110.

49. Rose, E.A., Porcerelli, J.H., and Neale, A.V. (2000) 'Pica: Common but commonly missed.' *Journal of American Board of Family Medicine 13*, 5, 353–358.

50. Miller, W.R. and Rellnich, S. (2012) *Motivational Interviewing*, Third Edition. New York: Guilford Press.

51. Bandura, A. (1977) *Social Learning Theory*. Englewood Cliffs, NJ: Prentice Hall.

52. Sacks, O. (1993) 'An Anthropologist on Mars.' *The New Yorker*. Available at www.newyorker.com/magazine/1993/12/27/anthropologist-mars, accessed on 25 July 2016.

53. Hahamy, A., Behrmann, M., and Malach, R. (2015) 'The idiosyncratic brain: Distortion of spontaneous connectivity patterns in autism spectrum disorder.' *Nature Neuroscience 18*, 302–309. doi: 10.1038/nn.3919.

54. The Graham Norton Show (2014) *Jamie Dornan's Weird Walk – The Graham Norton Show*. Available at www.youtube.com/watch?v=rSXr0LBdVzA, accessed on 25 July 2016.

55. Lombardo, M., Pierce, K., Eyler, L.T., Barnes, C.C., *et al.* (2015) 'Differential functional neural substrates for good and poor language outcome in autism.' *Neuron 86*, 2, 567–577. doi: 10.1016/j.neuron.2015.03.023.

56. Dike, C.C., Baranoski, M., and Griffith, E.E. (2005) 'Pathological lying revisited.' *Journal of American Academy of Psychiatry and the Law 33*, 3, 342–349.

57. Siegel, M., and Beaulieu, A.A. (2012) 'Psychotropic medications in children with Autism Spectrum Disorder: A systematic review and synthesis for evidence-based practice.' *Journal of Autism and Developmental Disorders 42*, 1592. doi: 10.1007/s10803-011-1399-2.

58. Sperling, G. (1960) 'The information available in brief visual presentations.' *Psychological Monographs: General and Applied 74*, 11, 1–29. doi: 10.1037/h0093759.

59. Maslow, A.H. (1966) *The Psychology of Science: A Reconnaissance*. Chapel Hill, NC: Maurice Bassett.

60. Gordon, A.M., Westling, G., Cole, K.J., and Johansson, R.S. (1993) 'Memory representations underlying motor commands used during manipulation of common and novel objects.' *Journal of Neurophysiology 69*, 6, 1789–1796.

61. Adams, T. (2013) 'Henry Molaison: the amnesiac we'll never forget.' *The Guardian*. Available at www.theguardian.com/science/2013/may/05/henry-molaison-amnesiac-corkin-book-feature, accessed on 25 July 2016.

62. Ozgen, H., Hellemann, G.S., Stellato, R.K., Lauhis, B., *et al.* (2011) 'Morphological features in children with autism spectrum disorder: A matched case-control study.' *Journal of Autism and Developmental Disorders 41*, 1, 23–31. doi: 10.1007/s10803-010-1018-7.

63. Castellanos, J., and Azelrod, D. (1990) 'Effect of habitual knuckle cracking on hand function.' *Annals of the Rheumatic Diseases: The Eular Journal 49*, 308–309. doi:10.1136/ard.49.5.308.

64. Voineagu, I., Wang, X., Johnston, P. Lowe, J.K., Tian, Y., and Horvath, S. (2011) 'Transcriptomic analysis of autistic brain reveals convergent molecular pathology.' *Nature 474*, 380–384. doi:10.1038/nature10110.

65. Pearce, N. (2012) 'Jessica-Jane Applegate becomes first intellectually disabled Brit to win gold at 2012 Paralympics Games.' *The Telegraph.* Available at www.telegraph.co.uk/sport/olympics/paralympic-sport/9516077/Jessica-Jane-Applegate-become-first-intellectually-disabled-Brit-to-win-gold-at-2012-Paralympic-Games.html, accessed on 25 July 2016.

66. Nordahl, C.W., Lange, N., Li, D.D., Barnett, L.A., *et al.* (2011) 'Brain enlargement is associated with regression in preschool-age boys with autism spectrum disorder.' *Proceedings of the National Academy of Sciences of the United States of America 11*, 50, 20195–20200. Available at www.pnas.org/cgi/doi/10.1073/pnas.1107560108, accessed on 25 July 2016.

67. Scott-van Zeeland, H.H., Abrahams, B.S., Alvarez-Retuerto, A.I., Sonnenblick, L.I., *et al.* (2010) 'Altered functional connectivity in frontal lobe circuits is associated with variation in the autism risk gene.' *Science Translational Medicine 2*, 5, 56–80. doi: 10.1126/scitranslmed.3001344.

68. Tang, G., Gudsnuk, K., Kuo, S-H., Cotrina, M.L., *et al.* (2014) 'Loss of mTOR-dependent macroautophagy causes autistic-like synaptic pruning deficits.' *Neuron 83*, 5, 1131–1143. doi: http://dx.doi.org/10.1016/j.neuron.2014.07.040.

69. Parikshak, N.N., Luo, R., Zhang, A., Won, H., *et al.* (2013) 'Integrative functional genomic analyses implicate specific molecular pathways and circuits in autism.' *Cell 155*, 5, 1008–1021. doi: 10.1016/j.cell.2013.10.031.

70. Royal Australian and New Zealand College of Psychiatrists (2016) *Psychologists and Psychiatrists: What's the Difference.* Available at www.ranzcp.org/Mental-health-advice/What-is-a-psychiatrist/Psychiatrists-and-psychologists.aspx, accessed on 25 July 2016.

71. Sinha, Y., Silove, N., Hayen, A., and Williams, K. (2011) 'Auditory integration therapy for autism spectrum disorder.' *Cochrane Database of Systematic Reviews 12*, CD003681. doi: 10.1002/14651858. CD003681.pub3.

72. Zane, T. (2011) 'Now hear this: How science and evidence won out against auditory integration therapies.' *The Current Repertoire: Newsletter of the Cambridge Centre for Behavioural Studies 24*, 1.

73. Mazurek, M.O., and Wenstrup, C. (2013) 'Television, video game and social media use among children with ASD and typically developing siblings.' *Journal of Autism and Developmental Disorders 43*, 6, 1258–1271. doi: 10.1007/s10803-012-1659-9.

74. Johnson, C.P., and Myers, S.M. (2007) 'Identification and evaluation of children with autism spectrum disorders.' *Paediatrics 120*, 5, 1183–1215. doi: 10.1542/peds.2007-2361.

75. Godlee, F., Smith, J., and Marcovitch, H. (2011) 'Wakefield's article linking MMR vaccine and autism was fraudulent.' *BMJ 342*. doi: http://dx.doi.org/10.1136/bmj.c7452.

76. Wakefield, A.J., Murch, S.H., Anthony, A., Linnell, J., *et al.* (1998) 'Ileal lymphoid nodular hyperplasia, non-specific colitis, and pervasive developmental disorder in children [retracted].' *Lancet 351*, 9103, 637–641.

77. Skinner, B.F. (1938) *The Behaviour of Organisms: An Experimental Analysis.* New York, NY: Appleton Century.

78. Pavlov, I.P. (1927) *Conditional Reflexes.* New York, NY: Dover.

79. Lovaas, O.I., Schreibman, L., Koegel, R., and Rehm, R. (1971) 'Selective responding by autistic children to multiple sensory input.' *Journal of Abnormal Psychology 77*, 3, 211–222. doi: 10.1037/h0031015.

80. Heffner, G.F. (n.d.) *The Autism Home Page.* Available at http://autism-help.org/behavior-out-of-control.htm, accessed on 3 August 2016.

81. Dickerson, P., Robins, B., and Dautenhahn, K. (2013) 'A conversation analytic perspective on interaction between a humanoid robot, a co-present adult and a child with an ASD.' *Interaction Studies 14*, 2, 297–316. doi: 10.1075/is.14.2.07dic.

82. Durand, V.M. (2002) 'Treating sleep terrors in children with autism.' *Journal of Positive Behaviour Interventions 4*, 2, 66–72. doi: 10.1177/109830070200400201.

83. Ming, X., Sun, Y-M., Nachajon, R.V., Brimacombe, M., and Walters, A.S. (2009) 'Prevalence of parasomnia in autistic children with sleep disorders.' *Clinical Medicine: Paediatrics 3*, 1–10. Available at www.ncbi. nlm.nih.gov/pmc/articles/PMC3676289/pdf/cped-3-2009-001. pdf, accessed on 25 July 2016.

84. Nilsson, P.M., Nilsson, J.A., Hedblad, B., and Berglund, G. (2001) 'Sleep disturbance in association with elevated pulse rate for prediction or mortality – consequences of mental strain.' *Journal of Internal Medicine* *250*, 6, 521–529. doi: 10.1046/j.1365-2796.2001.00913.

85. Tomlinson, J., Walker, E.A., Bujalska, I.J., Draper, N., *et al.* (2004) '11β-hydroxysteroid dehydrogenase Type 1: A tissue-specific regulator of glucocorticoid.' *Response Endocrine Reviews 25*, 5, 831–866. doi: 10.1210/er.2003-0031#sthash.07LPrbAN.dpuf.

86. Gray, C. (2010) *The New Social Story Book*. Arlington, TX: Future Horizons.

87. Bandura, A. (1977) *Social Learning Theory*. Englewood Cliffs, NJ: Prentice Hall.

88. Baron-Cohen, S. (1991) 'Precursors to a Theory of Mind: Understanding Attention in Others.' In A. Whiten (ed.) *Natural Theories of Mind: Evolution, Development and Simulation of Everyday Mindreading.* Oxford: Blackwell.

89. *Cochrane Database of Systematic Reviews (CDSR)* Available at www.cochranelibrary.com/cochrane-database-of-systematic-reviews, accessed on 25 July 2016.

90. Raspin, I. (2001) 'Autism Spectrum Disorder: Relevance to Tourette Syndrome.' *Advanced Neurology 85*, 89–101.

91. Dewar, G. (2016) *Parenting for the Science-Minded*. Available at www.parentingscience.com, accessed on 25 July 2016.

92. Time Timers (2016) Available at www.timetimer.com, accessed on 25 July 2016.

93. Grandin, T. (2006) *Thinking in Pictures: My Life with Autism*. New York, NY: Vintage Books.

Stephen Heydt has worked as a clinician in Australia and internationally since 1981, specialising in experiences of trauma as well as behavioural and cognitive difficulties. Having worked in conflict and post-conflict contexts, Stephen has also directed mental health services for 1.5 million refugees, some 140 mother and child health centres, covering six countries and some forty refugee camps for the United Nations. He now runs Healthy Minds, a specialist clinical practice in Brisbane, Australia.

'Stephen Heydt's love, respect and understanding of children on the autism spectrum shines through in this easily accessible book. It is a veritable cornucopia of all things pertaining to autism. Scrupulously researched, it makes finding information on all aspects of autism as easy as ABC.

A book that is Accessible, Beneficial and Convenient, that should grace the shelves of all those who are eager to know more about this enigmatic condition.'

— K. I. Al-Ghani, specialist advisory teacher, university lecturer,
autism trainer and international author of books on ASD

'"Each child's different qualities enrich us all," Stephen Heydt reminds readers in this brief but reassuring, wide-ranging guide. Practical and accessible, *A Parents' ABC of the Autism Spectrum* offers sympathetic, clear definitions, concise explanations, and thoughtful strategies for how we can best support our children with ASD.'

— Liane Kupferberg Carter, author of Ketchup is My Favorite
Vegetable: A Family Grows Up with Autism